BEYOND THE HORIZON

AN APPEAL TO PARENTS FOR CLASSICAL CHRISTIAN EDUCATION

Joe Ben House & Colton F. Moore

Foreword by

Louis Markos

GH

GlossaHouse
Wilmore, KY
GlossaHouse.com

Beyond the Horizon: An Appeal to Parents for Classical Christian Education

Published by GlossaHouse
110 Callis Circle
Wilmore, KY 40390

Publisher's Cataloging-in-Publication Data:

x, 184 pages ; 15.24 x 22.86 cm

ISBN: 978-1-63663-111-0

1. Non-Fiction, Christian. 2. Author. 3. I. Title. II. Series.

Library of Congress Control Number:

Cover Design by T. Michael W. Halcomb

Typeset by Colton F. Moore and Fredrick J. Long

The font used to create this work are available from www.linguistsoftware.com/lgku.htm

"It is a matter of great satisfaction to me to hope that my children will be in circumstances to receive a good education. Mine was defective and I feel the inconvenience, if not the misfortune of not receiving a classical education. Knowledge is the food of genius, and my son, let no opportunity escape you to treasure up knowledge."

—Sam Houston

Dedicated to Nicholas, TaraJane, Nathaniel, and Caroline—the four strongest proofs I know of for Classical Christian Education

And to Stephanie, my wife and the mother of our quartet, for putting a melody to all the labors of classical Christian Education.

—Joe Ben House

τῇ μου ἀγαπητῇ, σοὶ πρῶτον βιβλίον τοῦτο.

—Colton F. Moore

Foreword

I used to think that progressivism began its takeover of our public schools in the 1960s and 70s. I was wrong. That is not when it began, but when it reached its climax—most fully realized in the removal of the Bible and prayer from public schools. Since that climax, our schools have slipped further and further away from their classical and Christian roots, culminating with the acceptance and promotion of the transgender movement in school districts across the nation.

The takeover did not begin in the 1960s and 70s; it began a century earlier in the 1860s and 70s, in the aftermath of the Civil War. With the arrival in America of the Prussian educational theories of Humbolt, secular research took the place of liberal arts education grounded in virtue and the classics: the dominant model in the South until the North forced the Prussian model upon it. Meanwhile, the spread of the industrial revolution and of social Darwinism skewed education toward a vocational model that emphasized skills over character. New waves of immigration threw an additional burden of socialization on a public school system ill equipped for the task.

The original pledge of allegiance, written by Francis Bellamy in 1892, did not contain the words "under God"; those were added by President Eisenhower during the Cold War to distinguish America from the (literally) godless communism of the Soviet Union. The original pledge was meant to be a secular oath made to a secular flag. The patriotism it called for was not meant to strengthen the Judeo-Christian foundation of America but to offer a substitute for it.

This substitute religion, allied with a new vision of public schools as sites of vocational training, social engineering, and secular research, detached education from its traditional roots in classical languages and literature and the trivium of grammar, logic, and rhetoric. It further detached it from one of the chief goals of education: to properly train the affections, cultivate the virtues, and order the desires of students at various stages in their growth.

Only after considering carefully my public-school days in the 1970s and then factoring in data from my children's public education and the testimonies of my incoming freshmen did I become aware of something that lies at the heart of progressive education. In an unending parade, public schools have set themselves the task of inculcating in students fashionable, newly minted values that, though not necessarily bad or vicious, exist in opposition to traditional virtues of courage, temperance, wisdom, justice, honesty, hard work, loyalty, patience, thrift, faith, hope, and love.

Here, in rough chronological order, are some of the causes that public schools have pressed upon students over the last century: anti-drinking, anti-smoking, hygiene, evolution, family planning, feminism, safe-sex, environmentalism, tolerance, gay rights, multiculturalism, equity, diversity, identity politics, and transgenderism. Although, again, not all these causes are bad ones, they have never stood at the center of moral education. To the contrary, they have been taught in such a way as to drive a subtle wedge between the student and his church, his ethnic community, and his family. Rather than work in tandem with parents, progressive schools regularly teach students to feel morally superior to their superstitious, out-of-date, judgmental parents.

I applaud John Dewey and his fellow progressives for seeking to use the public school system as a conduit for integrating diverse ethnic immigrant communities into the melting pot of the United States. Unfortunately, rather than integrate them into the Greco-Roman, Judeo-Christian matrix out of which American was born, they resisted what they dubbed "fixed" or "ready-made" ideas that they felt needed to be subjected to the "scientific" reasoning of the Enlightenment. They wanted a strong and integrated America, but they wanted to change that America to fit their progressive ideas about the nature of man and society.

Thankfully for parents who want their students to be raised in a traditional educational system that takes seriously its calling to "pass down" (what *traditio* means in Latin) the classical Christian legacy that built this country and to instill the only virtues that can keep that legacy alive, an alternative to the public schools has arisen. I do not mean the many Catholic, Baptist, Episcopal, Methodist, and Lutheran schools that dot the landscape of America. Sadly, a goodly number of those faith-based institutions are simply public schools with chapels. Rather than seek to revive true, pre-Enlightenment classical education, most have simply followed the game plan of progressive public education and then sprinkled in some Bible stories and moral lessons.

The alternative of which I speak are consciously constituted classical Christian schools that reject the progressive theories of Dewey and his heirs and commit themselves to a rigorous, but joyous curriculum grounded in Latin, the trivium, the Great Books of the Western Intellectual Tradition, Socratic dialogue, a robust biblical worldview, and traditional morality and ethics. Some of these schools are full-time; others are part time "university model" schools where parents homeschool for three days a week and their children attend school in person on the other two days. All demand and receive buy-in from parents who want to raise virtuous, morally self-regulating citizens and not just cogs in a workplace that values only economic productivity, amoral consumerism, and an uncritical embrace of diversity, equity, and inclusion.

The book you hold in your hand offers a rich and breezy overview of the nature and methods of classical Christian education. I commend it to you as a guide to the kind of education that nurtured the true movers and shakers of the past—those who achieved excellence without sacrificing their souls, their families, or their sacred honor.

But beware, if you send your children to such a school—and I very much hope you will—do not think you are investing in a "college prep" school. If your children take seriously the education they will receive, they will be accepted, if not fought over, by college admissions offices. But that will not be the purposeful end—what the Greeks called a *telos*—toward which their education will lead them. What these schools are about is forming true ladies and gentlemen, young people who will love the Lord and who will possess wisdom, virtue, and eloquence.

Louis Markos, Professor in English and Scholar in Residence
Houston Christian University
Houston, Texas
Summer 2024

Table of Contents

An Excerpt From *Scott-King's Modern Europe*[1]

The headmaster: "You know we are starting this year with fifteen fewer classical specialists than we had last term"?

Scott-King: "I thought that would be about the number."

Headmaster: "As you know I'm an old Greats man myself. I deplore it as much as you do. But what are we to do? Parents are not interested in producing the 'complete man' anymore. They want to qualify their boys for jobs in the modern world. You can hardly blame them, can you"?

"Oh yes," said Scott-King. "I can and do."

Headmaster: "What I was going to suggest was—I wonder if you will consider taking some other subject as well as the classics? History, for example, preferably economic history"?

"No, headmaster."

"But, you know, there may be something of a crisis ahead." "Yes, headmaster."

"Then what do you intend to do"?

"If you approve, headmaster, I will stay as I am here as long as any boy wants to read the classics. I think it would be very wicked indeed to do anything to fit a boy for the modern world."

"It's a short-sighted view, Scott-King."

"There, headmaster, with all respect, I differ from you profoundly. I think it is the most long-sighted view it is possible to take."

---

[1] Reproduced in full from Evelyn Waugh, *Scott-King's Modern Europe* (Boston: Chapman & Hall, 1948), 88–89.

PART 1

WELCOME. WE'RE GLAD YOU'RE HERE.

Chapter One

HELP! WE HAVE CHILDREN!

I (Ben) was sitting in my office perusing a stack of unread books. Like the sirens in Homer's *Odyssey*, they were all inviting me to skip the daily tyrannies of school administration and just read. The quietness was broken when I heard the door to the administration offices open.

The first voice was Mrs. Harrison's cheerful words. As secretary, her job was to save me from too many interruptions and to make sure I actually did some real administrative work.

"Good morning. How are you doing"?

(She always set a good tone for people coming in for scheduled appointments.) I suspected already, however, that this was not going to be a good morning and that Joseph and Alicia Holmes were not doing well.

I continued shuffling a few papers on my desk and could hear the small talk between the married couple and my secretary. As they entered my office, I stood up and tried to be cheerful myself.

"Hello, Joseph ... Good morning, Alicia. Come on in and sit down."

Mrs. Harrison closed the door and left the three of us trapped in the office to confront some unpleasant matters. As long as I have been in this job, I still find it difficult to begin talking in these awkward meetings. So, I started with something neutral.

"That road construction on the loop is really making it difficult to get here."

Joseph and Alicia just nodded. I knew then there was no time or place for any small talk. We had to get straight to the point. Alicia had a wadded up Kleenex clinched in her hand. Her eyes looked somewhat puffy. I glanced around the office to make sure that I had a box of Kleenexes ready.

Joseph looked grim, almost angry, and uncomfortable. He glanced once or twice at the door as though he might bolt out.

"Well, let's get right down to business. But let's go ahead and begin with prayer."

Not knowing the problems and not even knowing Joseph and Alicia Holmes that well, I prayed what felt like a generic "one size fits all" prayer: "Lord, You know all things. You know our hearts, our troubles, and our needs. Give us wisdom and give Joseph and Alicia the answers and direction they need. In Christ's name we pray. Amen."

"Okay, what's on your minds"?

Silence—a long silence, and then a glance between the two of them. I was fearful there were some serious marital problems, or maybe financial problems, or perhaps some difficult moral issue. The silence was painful.

Alicia began to speak, but Joseph interrupted: "It's our kids. It's Joe, Jr. and Louisa Jane."

Having worked with children and families for many years, I imagined the range of problems that might be occurring.

Alicia then started talking, "Yes, it's our children. We have lost them. We cannot talk with them anymore. They are distant. They have changed. It has happened because of school—this school. It's the group that they have fallen in with. It's ..."

She could not go on. She choked up and began quietly sobbing. Joseph said, "Alicia is exactly right. They used to be so normal. They were good kids. We were so proud of them. We were being good parents. But now they aren't like they were. We cannot communicate with them."

Now Joseph was choked up. I edged the Kleenex box closer to where he was.

"The things they say ... the language they use ... the things they talk about," Alicia said between sobs. "They've gotten into things that ... well, even if they asked me, I don't even know how to help them."

"Alicia is right. We don't know what to say to them. I heard some of that kind of talk in college. But Benjamin Joseph—we call him Joe, Jr.—is only in tenth grade and Louisa Jane is a freshman," Joseph said.

I was struggling to take notes, trying to grasp the problem, and sympathize at the same time. But I still did not understand what it was that troubled them so.

"The music they listen to ..." Joseph continued. "And Joseph, Jr.'s language...."

A long painful pause.

Then Alicia spoke, "Both of them come home from school, go up to their rooms, close the door and we hardly see them in the evenings."

Alicia broke down again and Joseph reached over and took her hand.

Calmly and softly, I began.

"I know you are both hurting. You are not the first or only parents who are suffering from these kinds of things. This is not hopeless. But let's deal with some specifics. What is the language you are talking about? What did Joseph, Jr. say? And don't hold back."

Joseph answered, "I tried to talk with him. I admit on my part that I began yelling. I threatened to take away some of his privileges if he didn't change. And he said something I never expected to hear from my own son."

"Go ahead," I said, and Alicia was now holding Joseph's hand. It was difficult to watch a grown man in tears.

"He said, 'Dad ... your threats are ... an *ad baculum* fallacy.'" Joseph sunk his head in hands. Alicia put her arm around him.

Alicia looked up at me with a desperate look in her eye. "What are we going to do"?

I began a series of questions: "Do you think that the problems are caused by the school they attend"?

Both nodded.

"Are they using words you don't know and language you are not familiar with"?

Both nodded again.

"Doesn't it seem that a big part of this whole matter is spiritual? This isn't just who they are around, but something deeper." And then I added," I say that because I have seen this both as a pastor and teacher. We are talking about a spiritual and theological issue."

Both nodded again.

"Are they reading big books? Classics"?

Both nodded more forcefully, and Alicia said, "My own daughter wants to have a copy of Aristotle for her very own. And I found this Dos-toy … Dos-toy—"

"Dostoevsky"?

"Yes, that. It was hidden under Joseph, Jr.'s bed. He first said it was for school, and then he admitted that he was just reading it for fun."

"Tell them about the movie we caught them watching," Joseph said.

Alicia struggled to get control of herself and then began the story. The problem was not the movie itself, but the argument their children got into after it was over.

"Joe, Jr. kept saying that the story was exist-ist...extra stencilist philosophy. Then Louisa Jane was saying it wasn't. She was defending it because of some redemption thing about the ending. They just kept getting louder and louder. I admit, I lost it. I screamed out for them to stop. "Can't you two even watch a movie without all of this stuff going on"?

"It is happening more and more," Joseph jumped. "Movies, music, television, ads, whatever. They cannot let anything just slide by. It's ruining them."

Believe me, these were two very concerned, fearful, and worried parents. The painful part of counseling is coming to understand the problems. The cheerful part is knowing that there are answers. So, I was upbeat and comforting.

"Joseph, Alicia, I have seen this many times. You are going to be okay. I have seen this dozens of times. The condition your children have is Parents of Classically Christian Trained Children Syndrome.[2] Many, if not all, of the parents here at this school have been through this. You are going to get through this."

Alicia's face brightened up.

"Will we ever get our children back? Will things ever be the same? Will they ever be normal again"?

"No, never. As George Grant often says, 'They have been ruined.' Once they have read the classics, learned logic, experienced the greatest ideas of all time, and once they have learned how to learn, they will

---

[2] Commonly referred to as PCCTCS, which is hard to remember, so it is often not referred to by either the lengthy name or the initials.

never be the same. Your children will never be 'normal' by our country's standards."

Alicia's smile vanished.

"But what will they do? How will they live their lives"?

I leaned back in my chair. "They will go out, by God's grace, and change the world."

Yes, We Give Homework (Actually God Does)

This book is addressed to parents who are considering classical Christian education or already have their children in such a school. Education for your children is costly. Part of that cost is economic and it hits the pocketbook. The greater cost is that of commitment and faith in what is being done. Children are homework. They are the most important homework assignment you have. Parents are instructed to bring their children up in the nurture and admonition of the Lord (Ephesians 6:4). This does not mean to simply drop the kids off at Sunday school or unload them in the school parking lot.

Parents need help. They need the covenant community of the church, and, in many cases, the teaching skills and training of teachers. A computer helps with a writing assignment, but does not do the writing; likewise, a good church, good friends, and a good school can help, direct, and enhance good parenting. But you, the parents, still have homework.

We are going to give some assignments. Do them. You cannot pass this class without doing your homework. Tests? Your children are the tests. Along with the assignments, which are Bible passages to read, think, and pray over, we will be giving a few reading suggestions. We will exceedingly struggle to only list a few books. We love book lists and could devote pages to this, but it is best to start with a few reading assignments and work up from there.

Assignment for Chapter 1

Pray daily for your child's education, and pray for your parenting. The best school in the world cannot replace the work of the Holy Spirit in your child's heart. Therefore, don't expect education to fill in what duties you have as a parent. Pray for your children and their education.

Scripture Memorization

Proverbs 1:7:

> The fear of the LORD is the beginning of knowledge; fools despise wisdom and instruction.[3]

Recommended Reading Assignments

Voddie Baucham, *Family Driven Faith* (Wheaton, IL: Crossway, 2011).

---

[3] All Scripture translations use the *English Standard Version* (Wheaton, IL: Crossway, 2001).

Chapter Two

CHANGE THE WORLD (CHILDREN WELCOME)

Our children, by God's grace, are to go from the environment of our homes and change the world. That is a big assignment. God often gives impossibly large homework assignments. Consider the following: we are to pray for his will to be done on earth as it is in heaven (Matt 6:10). We are to be light to the world and salt to the earth. (Matt 5:13–15). We are to go and make disciples of all the nations (Matt 28:19).

These are astronomically challenging assignments—assignments that we cannot accomplish on our own. So, why does God give this kind of impossible-to-complete homework? He assigns such cosmic assignments because his very own power resides within us, the church (Eph 3:21). The church, though a singular noun, is comprised of countless individuals—individuals who share different gifts by the same Holy Spirit (1 Cor 12:4). The variety of God-bestowed gifts within the church actually serve each other on these cosmic homework assignments. Yes, you can and must work together. Our God is not a solitary being, but the triune God in whose image he created us. The great Three-in-One has brought us together in communion with himself. Therefore, because he declares his glory among the nations, we (plural) also are commissioned. We (plural) are salt and light. We (plural) are praying for and working for the Kingdom of God.

God also calls us to use the Book—the Bible. As one teacher, named Joshua, told his students, "Bring your Book to class." His exact words were "This Book of the Law shall not depart from your mouth, but you shall be careful to do according to all that is written in it. For then you will make your way prosperous [meaning, get your assignments done], and then you will have good success [*meaning, pass the test*]" (Joshua 1:8).

Along with working together and using the Book, God expects us to recruit help in completing the assignments. Paul explains this principle in Second Timothy 2:1–2. In verse 1, Paul tells Timothy, "You, therefore, my son, be strong in the grace of the Lord Jesus Christ." Timothy was Paul's eyes, ears, and hands in the church at Ephesus where he was sent. Paul delegated part of his homework as an apostle to his faithful student Timothy. Next, Paul tells him this: "And the things you have heard from me among many witnesses, commit these to faithful men who will teach others also" (2 Timothy 2:2). You could say that Paul told Timothy to read over his lecture notes and then find some new students to learn the same material. These students will then recruit more new students. It is a pyramid principle, whereby God "Christianizes" the world—where every single nation will hear the gospel (Matt 24:14). This is multi-generational mentoring discipleship. This is Christian education.

God gives the big, impossibly big, assignments to us. Then he sets us in a small corner of the earth to fulfill the assignment. God says to take the gospel to all nations, and so he places many of us in marriages where, after a time, these marvelous little creatures start showing up in our homes every year or so. They arrive incomplete; they have to be taught language and instructed in the ways of Christ. They have to be civilized as well, learning culture and manners. They also have to be potty trained and taught letters and numbers. Unlike baby birds which fly out of the nest within weeks of birth, our children grow and learn incredibly slowly.

God tells us to be world changers and then confines us to a mailing address, a local church, a community, and a supper table with little faces all around it. In a world of eight-billion people, God puts us face to face with somewhere between one and ten little people.

The Christian family is central to God's mission to fill the entire earth with his glory through the church (Gen 12:3; Acts 2:39). Christian family life calls for strong relationships between husbands and wives. Good marriages are the heart of a spiritually-thriving home; they are the heartbeat of the home. (If you want your children to grow up with fond memories of their childhood, nurture your marriage first and foremost.) Christian family life calls for wise, godly parenting practices.

The defining term that explains your life in regard to your children's lives is "therefore." Our children are our "therefore." They live out the implications of what we have said, and even more important, lived out in front of them. Your children will absorb, imbibe, smooth-out, roughen up, build upon, or reject the world in which you raise them. Their lives will say, "My mother and father were like *that*; therefore, I am like *this*." That is both scary and hopeful.

In Ephesians 6:4, Paul tells fathers to raise their children in a Christian culture: "Bring them up in the discipline and instruction of the Lord." "Discipline" and "instruction" are good words. The first word in the original Greek is *paideia*, whose range of meaning encompasses not only "discipline" and even "instruction" but a general "upbringing." *Paideia* suggests a culture created by perpetual instruction, discipline, exhortation, guidance, and all-around shepherding. *Paideia* refers to the shaping of all the critical aspects of our children's lives. It is the creation and sustenance of the spiritual, physical, and intellectual atmosphere our children breathe. In another words, you could say that *paideia* is true education in its broadest sense. A home's *paideia* begins with the centerpiece of the home: the parents.[1] Are we submitting to and growing in the Lord's *paideia* for our lives? Are we pouring into our own local church? Is our church pouring into us? Daily investment into the Scriptures, weekly participation in the Eucharist, [2] and regular

---

[1] Believe it or not, your children are not the most important aspect of your family. Under Jesus' lordship *you the parents* are the focal point of the family. A classical education doesn't focus on the "blood flow" of education; rather, it emphasizes the *heartbeat* of education. If you have a good heartbeat, you'll have good blood flow. So it is with the family: if you nurture a strong, healthy marriage, you'll necessarily provide a godly context for your children to thrive.

[2] The Eucharist, otherwise known as Communion or The Lord's Supper, is an old term that refers to the Greek word εὐχαριστία (*eucharistia*), which means "thanksgiving." The idea is that whenever Christians partake of the wine and bread together, we render *thanksgiving* to God for the gospel that has saved and united us together.

confession of sins to one another all play a crucial part in the *paideia* of our own children.[3]

Children should be brought up in a Christian world. They should be engulfed Christian thought, prayers, and practice. By God's grace alone, their faith in God's gospel will be the locus from which all of their holy desires and ambitions flow. Preferably, our Christianity will impact our children's books, music, conversations, and companions. Christian principles will affect their career choices, the men and women whom they choose in marriage, and every corner of life.

Again, by God's grace alone our children are our "therefores," and they will live beyond our lives and go well beyond where we have been. One author titled his book *Ideas have Consequences*.[4] So do children. So does education—especially education (*paideia*). Our goal should be that our children will stand on our shoulders, that they will see farther than we see, that they will go farther than we have gone. They will not only see the horizon toward which we have pointed them, but they will, by standing on our shoulders, see beyond the horizon to which we have pointed them.

We parents can benefit from what John of Salisbury in the 12th century said of his own teacher, Bernard of Chartres:

> Our own generation enjoys the legacy bequeathed to it by that which preceded it. We frequently know more, not because we have moved ahead by our own natural ability, but because we have been supported by the [mental] strength of others, and possess riches that we have inherited

---

[3] In the classical Christian school world, there are terms, authors, books, and ideas that show up repeatedly. The more you learn about the classical Christian movement, the more you become familiar with all of these. One such word is *paideia*, which is pronounced as "pie-day-uh." The classic and hefty work on the subject is Werner Jaeger's *Paideia: The Ideals of Greek Culture*, 3 vols. (Oxford: Oxford University Press, 1945). His work highlights how extensive the Greek influence was from the ancient to the modern world. Ideas have consequences (an oft-used phrase), and it is the culture of an age that always triumphs over politics and other trends.

[4] Richard M. Weaver, *Ideas Have Consequences* (Chicago: Chicago University Press, 1948).

> from our forefathers. Bernard of Chartres used to compare us to [puny] dwarfs perched on the shoulders of giants. He pointed out that we see more and farther than our predecessors, not because we have keener vision or greater height, but because we are lifted up and borne aloft on their gigantic stature.[5]

The formation of our children begins within the home; *paideia* begins with parents. And here is the good news, parents: *you cannot do the homework God has assigned you.* God gives work too difficult, too great, for us. There is not enough time, nor do we have the capacity or the abilities needed. Again, this is good news. Why?

"Without me, you can do nothing," said our Lord (John 15:5). If no other area of life brings us to realize the truth of what Jesus has said, raising children will. We must be faithful parents. We must "bring them up in the *paideia* and instruction of the Lord" (Ephesians 6:4). This especially includes formal education; this includes school.

We must secure the best education for our children. *But how we define "best" determines everything for our children's education.* School for our children is not about social status. It is not about financial ease. It is not about getting a prestigious college scholarship or high paying job, although either or both have their benefits. It is not about extra-curricular activities.

The most important thing about school, which is often overlooked, is that *school is primarily about education.* That is, it is about *paideia*—upbringing. Have you ever commented on a restaurant after a meal by saying, "It was great except for the food"? Obviously, if a restaurant fails in the food area, it has a big problem. If Mordor High School has great sports programs and facilities, if it has a plethora of course offerings, if it is just two blocks away and free, but it does not educate,

---

[5] As quoted by Richard M. Gamble, *The Great Tradition: Classic Readings on What It Means to be an Educated Human Being* (Wilmington, DE: ISI Books, 2009), xviii.

it is not a school. That is, if *paideia* isn't the primary concern of the school, then it has no business masquerading as that which it isn't.

We have plenty to discuss regarding proper schooling; just keep reading. For now, remember the great amount of homework God has given you, and give thanks for the helpers he sends—your children.

Assignment for Chapter 2

Using Matthew 28:18–20, the Great Commission, pray over this passage, apply it to your children's future, and consider how this might shape *your* family. What hath missions to do with child-rearing?

Scripture Memorization

Proverbs 22:6:

> Train up a child in the way he should go; even when he is old he will not depart from it.

Recommended Reading Assignments

Douglas Wilson, "The Paideia of God" in *The Paideia of God and Other Essays on Education* (Moscow, ID: Canon Press, 1999).

CHAPTER THREE

THE EDUCATIONAL SUPER HIGHWAY

What is education? What is education *for*? The answers to these two questions govern every expectation we have of any school.

Consider this definition: education is transportation. When all else fails in a discussion, resort to metaphors. They work because poetry defines truth more exactly than technical, precise answers do. Metaphors are like rocks and rivers, while technical and precise explanations are abstractions. That is true, unless the technical and exact definition uses metaphors. (Is your head spinning yet?)

Education is transportation. Think of all the kinds of transportation, all the ways that we use transportation, and all the content of the word transportation, and then you can start applying these ideas to education. Most importantly, transportation is a means of getting somewhere you currently are not. Transportation takes us "there and back again," as Bilbo would say. It takes us across the world or across the street. It leads us to opportunity, or it leads us to disaster.

To give a favorable nod to transportation, to say "I believe in transportation," is to say little or nothing. To use the phrase "excellence in transportation" sounds noble but means little. An airplane is excellent transportation for getting from Chicago to Hong Kong. But a horse with bits is better for traversing the vast, mountainous cattle ranches in Southern California. To get back to or to get away from the old ways of transportation can be good, bad, or indifferent, depending on the context. Transportation means nothing until we decide where we desire to travel. The favored mode of transportation depends upon how vital the trip experience itself is.

Where do you want your children's education to take them? Parents, you must wrestle with this question, and answer honestly. The quick Sunday school answer is "Jesus," and that is a good answer. We want our children to be Christians. In that light, we would be thankful if a straying child, a prodigal son or daughter, were to confess their sins and call upon Christ upon their deathbeds. Yet, our goal is not that our children return home like the prodigal son or to accept Christ like the thief on the cross. We do want prodigals to return, and we do want thieves on crosses to come to Christ! However, we have higher hopes for our children. We want to see them growing in the knowledge of Christ, relying on his great mercy and grace all the days of their lives.

We want our children to be with Christ in Paradise when they die, but we do not want them to be overly surprised at the scenery when they get there. Day one in heaven should not have to be spent learning hymns, learning how to praise God, and acknowledging the grace and mercy of Christ. Life and worship—one thing, not two—are to prepare us for the ultimate communion with God.

"*Thy Kingdom come. Thy will be done on earth as it is in heaven*" (Matt 6:10). This prayer is not a call to passivity as if we are telling God, "God, this one is totally in your hands. I am not helping." Rather "Thy will be done on earth as it is in heaven" is an active commission: "Lord, make us the instruments who make earth respond to the will, word, and Law of God to the same degree as heaven does." It is an enlistment and a commitment to put feet to the prayer.

So we ask again, where do you want your children's education to take them? As we all know, you cannot go west to get to the East. (Actually, you can, but that involves a long trip all the way around the world.) As parents who are thinking about where we want our children to go, which includes where we want our children's education to go, we need to stop thinking about our pocketbooks. *There*—our cards are out on the table. All too often, our thinking ends up sounding like this:

> *Parent*: "I really like the worldview and Christian values of Christian education."
> *Hidden Voice*: "Private school costs anywhere from four to ten thousand dollars a year."

> *Parent*: "We have such fine teachers in our school. And our kids can be a witness there."[1]

Education (*paideia*) and the multitude of costs that children entail begin at procreation. If you have children, you pay money. Want to save money? Don't have children. The issue is not one of economics. The issue is where do you want the transportation to take your children?

In this book, we are not primarily trying to convince public school-supporting Christians to change their views, although we will focus on that briefly. We do think that Christian parents sending their children to public schools is a serious matter with which each family must grapple.

Parents, if you are struggling between private Christian education and secularized public government schooling, keep struggling. I (Ben) taught for 16 years in public school and had lots of good teaching experiences, and I (Colton) currently teach Literature and Composition in a fantastic public school.[2] We know Christian teachers in public schools, we have had Christian students in our public school classrooms. Thank God for the salt and light in our government schools!

Let's use a comparison here to explain our point. In prisons all across the nation there are Christians. Whether some are there shamefully suffering for doing evil (1 Peter 3:17) or whether God has converted some there is beside the point; in prisons, to some degree or another, you will find Christ-followers. Some are guards while other are prisoners, and inevitably Christians in prison will witness to non-Christians. All of that being true, we do not want our children in prison—even a prison with a Christian warden and Christian guards and an active chapter of Chuck Colson's Prison Fellowship ministries. Why?

---

[1] This is true! Christian children are an incredible witness to non-believing students. But our point is this: education—*paideia*, upbringing and preparation—is training ground for the child. We train our children in-house *before* sending them out as witnesses whenever they leave the home. And besides, if your child goes to a private classical Christian school, he or she will have ample opportunities for reaching the lost during everyday circumstances (runs to the grocery store, play dates with neighborhood friends, church-led evangelism efforts, etc.).

[2] We are praying God might raise up a classical Christian school in our North-East Texas community.

Because prison is not an ideal setting in which children thrive and grow in the knowledge and wisdom of the Lord Christ. We want our children to be nurtured, surrounded, and nearly suffocated with Christian influences—and you cannot find such a Bible-saturation in our government schools.

Contrary to what many may believe, we want our children "sheltered" in a Christian home. We believe Christian parents have the obligation to envelop their children in a Christian culture. But we do not believe those Christian surroundings themselves can save our children.

Private classical Christian education cannot guarantee to deliver your child's soul to Jesus. Your child might find Christ in public school, prison, the mall, or even in church. Some kids who graduate from classical Christian schools abandon the faith. Some children who make A's in a classical Christian school Bible classes become apostate. A classical Christian school is not the gospel, nor is it, nor can it be, the Holy Spirit. If it were either, the tuition costs would soar.

A classical Christian school cannot necessarily and does not try to replace bad parenting or dysfunctional home lives. Teachers may serve as spiritual fathers and mothers at school, but they cannot be a substitute parent in the home. Nor can it replace the church and your pastors who "are keeping watch over your souls, as those who will have to give an account" (Heb 13:17).

Christian schools also cannot correct many students' learning or behavioral problems they may have had in previous schools. We are not reform schools. We can offer help, hope, and prayers for parents whose children have real and severe learning or behavioral problems. What we cannot offer to parents of problem children is an admittance application to our schools. If a ninth grader reads at a fourth grade level, giving him Fagles' translation of the *Iliad* instead of Lattimore's translation will probably not help. And the kid who hung around party animals in his previous school will not likely fit in with kids who are irked that Thomas Aquinas relied too heavily on Aristotle.

So, this transportation issue is complicated. Classical Christian schooling is not the cure for bad family life, nominal Christianity, learning problems, behavior problems, or other issues. We know there are hurting children and hurting parents who want answers. They, or you, need to get engulfed in a sound, Bible-saturated church, get Christian counseling, and start working on the root problems first.

Now for those who are waiting at this bus stop, because you are convinced of classical Christian education, we will now prepare you for the next crossroads: classical Christian education or other traditional methods of Christian education. This is not a battle between Christians and lions. There is a battle, but Christians with different approaches to Christian education are allies and brothers, not enemies.

We know this whole chapter has been built around the transportation metaphor. Now we have mixed metaphors and am talking about battles and warfare. The *Aeneid* is not the *Odyssey*, so we need to move away from singing of "warfare and a man of war" and back to the journey and that "man skilled in all ways of contending, the wanderer." In other words, it is time for a new chapter.

Assignment for Chapter 3

Using Deuteronomy 6:4–9, pray over this passage and with pen and paper in hand, write down at least three practical ways you could visibly demonstrate this passage in your home with your children. Consider the formal, structured implications of this text and the informal, spontaneous implications.

Scripture Memorization

Deuteronomy 6:4–9:

> Hear, O Israel: The LORD our God, the LORD is one. You shall love the LORD your God with all your heart and with all your soul and with all your might. And these words that I command you today shall be on your heart. You shall teach them diligently to your children, and shall talk of them when you sit in your house, and when you walk by the way, and when you lie down, and when you rise. You shall bind them as a sign on your hand, and they shall be as frontlets between your eyes. You shall write them on the doorposts of your house and on your gates.

Recommended Reading Assignments

C. S. Lewis, *The Abolition of Man* (Oxford: Oxford University Press, 1943).

Bradley Heath, *Millstones & Stumbling Blocks: Understanding Education in Post-Christian America* (Tuscon, AZ: Fenestra, 2006).

Samuel L. Blumenfield, *Is Public Education Necessary?* (Powder Springs, GA: American Vision, 2011).

Chapter Four

TIME FOR A HISTORY LESSON

Right in the middle of the floor of the library, there it was. It was all splayed out, whether done in haste or in expectation of being found. It was a manuscript that referred to obscure things, such as the trivium, grammar, logic, and rhetoric. It even referred to oddities such as the question of how many angels could dance on the head of a pin.

On close reading, it appeared to be a map of sorts: a map into the past, and yet also a map for the future. Whoever wrote it seemed to think not many would notice it, and it was many years before those papers were rediscovered, read, and tried.

The essay was entitled "The Lost Tools of Learning," written by an English woman who was not a teacher, who was not even a good parent, and who was mostly concerned with other types of writings other than education. And yet, that is exactly who it was. A chain smoker, a woman who birthed her only child illegitimately, who was married to an alcoholic, who had been a precocious auto-didactic child herself, who was a friend to such luminaries as C. S. Lewis and J. R. R. Tolkien, and who was an author of both Lord Peter Wimsey mysteries and theological writings. Not a saint by a long shot, Dorothy Sayers nonetheless is the godmother, the midwife, and the guardian angel of the rebirth of the classical Christian school movement on a continent across the pond from where she lived.[1]

Dorothy Sayers was a British woman who lived from 1893 to 1957. The expectations and sensibilities of the times were different then. She grew up as the child of an Anglican minister and was schooled in the British educational system, generally through the routes that were

---

[1] For more about Sayers, there are numerous biographies one may consult. We recommend Barbara Reynolds, *Dorothy L. Sayers: Her Life and Soul* (New York: St. Martin's Press, 1997).

permissible for females. At the same time, like a lot of original and creative thinkers, she bucked the system and stepped over many boundaries. She was both rebel and Christian, often in the same manner.

Neither she, nor C. S. Lewis (her friend), nor J. R. R. Tolkien (her contemporary) ever talked about starting Christian schools or pulling children out of public schools.[2]Their cultural setting was different from ours. Much of the language we use, the concepts we wrestle with, and the issues we face are American twenty-first century matters. We glean from the past, even the recent past, but we cannot graph the exact patterns of the past on our current situations because although truth does not change, how we speak of truth does.

Language and ideas have a cultural context. Again, truth does not change, but the way we express ideas does. For example, our history and government textbooks often use the word "democracy" when describing the beliefs and goals of our Founding Fathers. In contrast, our Founding Fathers disdained the word "democracy" and feared the consequences of creating such a government. (Note that the original Constitution allows only one democratically elected branch of government—the House of Representatives. And even there, voting rights were a State, not a national, determination.) Similarly, if someone 50 years ago says, "I got saved at a Billy Graham rally," another in their 80s will understand exactly what he or she is talking about. Or, if today someone says, "I accepted Jesus as my personal Lord and Savior," the language is familiar to a 30-year-old evangelical.

But someone from the 1600s and early 1700s would be as puzzled by that wording as they would if they heard the words "He texted me from his iPhone." In the past, Christians might refer to a salvation experience saying, "The Lord began to quicken my religious sensibilities." All of this reminds us that language has a context that often changes across time and cultures, although it does not mean that truth changes across time and cultures.

---

[2] See Louis Markos, *C. S. Lewis: An Apologist for Education* (Camp Hill, PA: Classical Academic Press, 2015).

Part One: Classical Christian Education

Classical education has a long, multi-varied, and rich history. It is rooted in the intersection in Christian culture of Judeo-Christian thought acclimating, borrowing from, and modifying Greco-Roman culture. For practical purposes, picture a student reading the Old and New Testament books alongside Homer, Plato, Aristotle, and Cicero.[3] Picture the student in late fourth century North Africa; call his name Augustine, or Austin for short. Educated in what we consider the "classics," but what he would probably only consider "books," Augustine became a Christian later in his life and applied his education to his theological writings and sermons for the church.[4]

Augustine stood between the Ancient and Medieval worlds, meaning he thought through, absorbed, criticized, swallowed whole, or wrote about the good, the bad, and the ugly from ancient thought. Along with Boethius (6th-century AD), Peter Abelard (12th-century AD), Thomas Aquinas (13th-century), and others, these transitional Christian thinkers and intellectual trailblazers became the teachers of the Medieval period. In other words, they wrote the curriculum guides that were used for the millennium between 500 and 1500 A.D.[5]

The patterns, models, and texts of education were never set in concrete, but educational methods were not guided by weather vanes either (and especially not Friday Night Lights or Dual-Credit courses). Medieval schools were not bothered by having old fashioned and truly old books that guided instruction. Tradition was education, and the Church was tradition. Moderated innovation was never scorned, but it had guidelines within which it worked. One could advance new ideas as long as they were rooted in and growing out of old ideas.

---

[3] See Louis Markos, *Myth Made Fact: Reading Greek and Roman Mythology through Christian Eyes* (Camp Hill, PA: Classical Academic Press, 2015); idem., *From Achilles to Christ: Why Christians Should Read the Pagan Classics* (Downers Grove, IL: IVP Academic, 2007).

[4] See Peter Brown, *Augustine of Hippo: A Biography*, rev. ed. (Oakland, CA: University of California, 2000)

[5] Thomas Cahill, *How the Irish Saved Civilization* (New York: Anchor Books, 2010).

Time for a History Lesson

The Protestant Reformers were trained in classical education. For example, John Calvin started off his academic career by writing a defining study of Seneca, a Roman philosopher who served under Nero.[6] Latin and Greek languages, logic, and reading the "classics" were not parts of education: they *were* education.[7] The same pattern was found in Britain and the same pattern migrated across the Atlantic to the twenty plus British colonies, of which a baker's dozen morphed into the United States.[8]

Classical education is not Christian *per ipse* (that's Latin for "in [or through] itself"); vain is the search for a model for classical education in the Holy Scriptures. It is, however, an ancient method of instruction and learning, dating back to the Romans and Greeks, and perhaps even to the Hebrews. It is called "classical" because of its antiquity and the general "catholicity" it enjoyed for centuries in the West as an educational exemplar (or perhaps even just "the norm").

When Christianity began to take over Europe, it brought its classical education with it—which included lots of Christian texts among the pagan Greeks and Latins. An unbeliever in the 16th–19th centuries, and in many cases the early 20th century (which itself was defaced by the progressive educational movements of John Dewey and even the ideas of the 19th-century ideas of Horace Mann), who was classically educated would likely have read the Old Testament in Hebrew, the New Testament in Greek, and Augustine and Thomas Aquinas in Latin. In an age where the idea of Google Translate would have been laughable, schools prioritized and enjoyed the ancient languages.

The modern American classical Christian school movement borrows lots of ideas from classical education. These borrowings include teaching Latin, reading lots of Greek and Roman pagan works, and

---

[6] Nero was the Roman emperor from 54 AD–68 AD.

[7] See Ronald B. Begley and Joseph W. Koterski, S. J., eds., *Medieval Education* (New York: Fordham University Press, 2005).

[8] The books you could read on the history of classical education are legion. We recommend two: *Good-by, Mr. Chips* by James Hilton (an enjoyable fictional account of classical education) and *Surprised by Joy* by C. S. Lewis (an autobiographical account).

reading lots from more recent classically trained people, particularly C. S. Lewis, Dorothy Sayers, T. S. Eliot, Louis Markos, Christopher Perrin, Douglas Wilson, and others. Modern classical Christian education gleans from, but does not make exact copies of older forms of classical education. Modern classical Christian education gleans from Greek and Roman pagans, but does not exalt them or canonize them in a way that only Scripture is canonized. Modern classical Christian education plunders the ancient pagans just as Israel plundered Pharoah's gold (Exod 3:22). Our student Augustine is helpful here:

> Like the treasures of the ancient Egyptians, who possessed not only idols and heavy burdens which the people of Israel hated and shunned but also vessels and ornaments of silver and gold, and clothes, which on leaving Egypt the people of Israel, in order to make better use of them, surreptitiously claimed for themselves ... similarly all the branches of pagan learning contain not only false and superstitious fantasies and burdensome studies that involve unnecessary effort, which each one of us must loathe and avoid as under Christ's guidance we abandon the company of pagans, but also studies for liberated minds which are more appropriate to the service of the truth, and some very useful moral instruction, as well as the various truths about monotheism to be found in their writers.[9] (*Doct. chris.* 2.40)

Thar's gold in thar' pagan hills.[10] And so, we mine the gold and toss away the dirt. The pagans excellently taught how to educate, and Christ truly shows us the beginning of education: the fear of the Lord.[11]

---

[9] All quotations of Augustine's *On Christian Teaching* are taken from Augustine, *De Doctrina Christiana*, ed. and trans. R. P. H. Green (Oxford: Clarendon, 1995).

[10] Many ascribe this phrase (minus the "pagan") to the 19th-century American miner and geologist N. F. Stephenson in 1849.

[11] For example, Daniel and Nebuchadnezzar. Notice that Daniel refused to eat the food of Babylon but had no qualms gleaning from their literature and language.

Part Two: Going Mutch Dutch

The modern classical Christian education movement in the United States has borrowed heavily from the ideas and labors of the Dutch Christian thinker, author, theologian, and educator Abraham Kuyper (1837–1920). This paragraph by Kuyper might in fact summarize his life and ministry:

> One desire has been the ruling passion of my life. One high motive has acted like a spur upon my mind and soul. And sooner than that I should seek escape from the sacred necessity that is laid upon me, let the breath of life fail me. It is this: that in spite of all worldly opposition, God's holy ordinances shall be established again in the home, in the school and in the State for the good of the people; to carve as it were into the conscience of the nation the ordinances of the Lord, to which Bible and Creation bear witness, until the nation again pays homage to God.[12]

This same philosophy, life mission, has been summarized in the most often quoted Kuyper statement: "There is not a square inch in the whole domain of human existence over which Christ, who is Sovereign over all, does not cry: Mine!"[13] Kuyper strongly believed in and was committed to Christian education.

His best book on Christian worldview thinking is *Lectures on Calvinism*—a series of lectures presented in 1898 at Princeton University at the invitation of Benjamin Breckinridge Warfield, a prominent theologian and president of Princeton Seminary. Abraham Kuyper was such a big name when he visited America that he was received at the White House and at numerous gatherings across the country.

The Calvinism that Kuyper talks about is not focused on whether your church or personal beliefs are in line with the theological tradition

---

[12] Abraham Kuyper, *Lectures on Calvinism* (Grand Rapids: Eerdmans, 1978), iii.

[13] As quoted in James D. Bratt, ed., *Abraham Kuyper: A Centennial Reader* (Grand Rapids, Eerdmans, 1998), 488.

associated with all the Johns: Calvin, Knox, Edwards, Witherspoon, Machen, Murray, MacArthur, and Piper. Kuyper was using the word "Calvinism" to represent the Protestant idea of all areas of life falling under the sovereign rule of God. His audience at Princeton understood the concept.

Kuyper described what he called a "Life and World System." That phrase has been shaped up in the years that followed to the term "Worldview" or "Christian Worldview." In terms of Christian education, it means this: a Christian school should not just have chapel and a Bible class and then approach every other subject just as secular schools do. Rather, a Christian school builds upon a Christian worldview—a Christian way of thinking and applying the faith—that is applied in every classroom, every subject, and every situation in school from playground activities to terminating employees.[14]

Kuyper and another Dutchman named Guillaume Groen van Prinsterer labored in politics, church circles, and society to create Christian schools in the Netherlands. They waged an eighty-year war against secularism and for the heart and souls of Christian families and children. Christian schools, Christian textbooks, and Christian teachers were the results of their labors in the Netherlands. Throughout the 1800s and again after World War II (1945), large numbers of Dutch people migrated to North America. Most were Christian, many were nurtured in the ideals of Kuyper, and they established Christian schools modeled after their old world experiences. Most of these Dutch immigrants settled in the northern and mid-western states, such as Indiana, Michigan, Iowa, and some settled parts of Canada.[15]

---

[14] Yes, there is a godly way to fire an employee. Consider these two articles: Darren Carlson, "How to Dismiss an Employee in a Church or Ministry," *The Gospel Coalition*, 6 July 2023, https://www.thegospelcoalition.org/article/dismiss-employee/; Brad Larson, "How to Lay Off Someone Like Jesus Would," *The Gospel Coalition*, 3 February 2020, https://www.thegospelcoalition.org/article/fire-someone-jesus/.

[15] Henry Stephen Lucas, *Netherlanders in America: Dutch Immigration to the United States and Canada, 1789–1950* (Ann Arbor: University of Michigan Press, 1955); James Dr. Bratt, *Dutch Calvinism in Modern America: A History of a Conservative Subculture* (Grand Rapids: Eerdmans, 1984).

Christian education had become engrained within the Dutch culture. Christ-centered education was the expectation. Their communities had Christian schools long before prayer was banned in public schools, long before integration issues created strife in public schools, and long before battles came to the forefront over the lack of certain educational programs (like phonics) or the addition of other programs (like sex education).

The American classical Christian education movement has borrowed heavily from the ideas of Abraham Kuyper. In particular, Kuyper's emphasis on the sovereignty of Christ over every subject and his emphasis on the conflict between Christian and non-Christian thought are part of the classical Christian school philosophy. We have, therefore, taken mutch from the Dutch.

Part Three: The Battle for the Bible

The third area where the modern Classical Christian school movement picked up its framework was from old Princeton. By "old Princeton," we mean Princeton University and Princeton Theological Seminary as they existed from their founding until the 1920s. During the first quarter or more of the twentieth century, the most important battle for the culture and soul of America was being fought. It was not being battled in Hollywood (this was when movies were only beginning to be made), or on Wall Street, or in the halls of Congress. If there is a geographical center to the culture war of the 1910s and 1920s, it was at Princeton Theological Seminary in New Jersey.

The main warrior for the cause of historic, orthodox Christianity was J. Gresham Machen. The primary weapon he created was a book called *Christianity and Liberalism*, which was and still is one of the most important books of the twentieth century. Machen ferociously attacked theological liberalism, not political liberalism.[16] He was opposed to both a denial of historic Christianity and the obtrusive expansion of the civil government that eventually forced fundamental Christianity to retreat

---

[16] J. Gresham Machen, *Christianity and Liberalism* (New York: Macmillan Company, 1923).

from the town square, from city hall, and from the school houses. It became a cultural assumption that politics and religion don't mix.

Much of the history of Bible-believing Christianity in America during the twentieth century falls under three slightly overlapping subheadings: Fundamentalism, Evangelicalism, and Calvinism. Since we are tossing big words out here and there, we can go ahead and mention some other words that were the battleground issues among American churches and society: Theological Liberalism (and the Higher Critical Movement), Neo-Orthodoxy and Darwinian Naturalism. Okay, we should all feel better for having used some big words.[17]

But this isn't the occasion to simply boast of pompous sounding words. Words represent ideas, which, as you now know, have consequences. Most of the theological history of American Christianity does not show up in history textbooks. If religion does show up, it is often portrayed as being in conflict with science and modernity. World Wars I and II, the Great Depression, the New Deal, and the Cold War are all focal points of twentieth century history, and rightly so, but the theological wars were arguably more important, or at least just as important as the political and foreign wars. The basic, historic, orthodox, and creedal doctrines came under attack. Some attacks came from the academic community, but most came within the Christian community.

Fundamentalism grew out of a defense of what were called the *Fundamentals of the Faith*.[18] These included the following:

1. The Biblical inspiration and inerrancy of the Scriptures
2. The virgin birth of Jesus Christ
3. The vicarious death of Jesus Christ for sin (otherwise known as substitutionary atonement)
4. The bodily resurrection of Jesus Christ
5. The miracles of Jesus Christ and of the Bible

---

[17] The best book on this topic is George M. Marsden, *Fundamentalism and American Culture* (Oxford: Oxford University Press, 2006).

[18] *The Fundamentals: A Testimony to the Truth*, 12 vols. (Chicago: Testimony Publishing Company, 1910–15).

These core beliefs, which hopefully you and your church unquestionably affirm, were being reinterpreted, denied, and rejected by opponents both from outside and inside the church. The term Theological Liberalism refers to the movement that rejected and attacked the Fundamentals.

Much of the controversy was related to the educational, social, political, and theological implications of Darwinian Naturalism. Charles Darwin's books had created a firestorm of controversy from the time of their publication (in the late 1850s) and on through the 20th century. Unlike later battles, these fights were not over Six Day Creation versus Evolution. Much of the controversy was over what a Naturalistic, as opposed to Supernaturalistic, view of God, man, and history would mean.

In agreement with the Fundamentals of the Faith, but adhering more to the wider teachings of Reformed theology, Calvinists were some of the most engaged warriors in this culture war. This brings us back to the role played by John Gresham Machen and his book Christianity and Liberalism. Machen's war was with writings, teachings, and actions. He and others left Princeton Theological Seminary, which had historically been the seedbed for American Presbyterianism and Calvinism. He also left the Presbyterian Church of the United States. Machen and his followers formed Westminster Theological Seminary and the Orthodox Presbyterian Church.

The influence of Machen's convictions has been much greater than the organizations he founded. He was spearheading a battle that involved more than just Presbyterians. It was, as stated above, a battle for the theological heart and soul of the nation. Many Bible believing Christians, pastors, and churches have been impacted by Machen, and in many cases, they don't know him and they would not agree with many points in his theological outlook.

Machen's wars were strategic retreats. He tenaciously clung to orthodox doctrines and Biblical convictions. When such tenets cost him his position in his seminary and church, he pulled back and started anew. In his time, his defense of the faith might have looked like a last stand or a desperate holding action. But the receding waves of the faith would be followed, in time, by a surge forward.

For over fifty years, that surge forward has been happening in America. Evangelicalism, that is, Bible believing Christianity with an emphasis on conversion, has proven to be a major component of American life. We would grant that the story of Evangelical Christianity is a complex tale of victories and defeats, advances and retreats, clarity and confusion, and mountain top experiences along with lots of valleys. Nevertheless, there are lots of Christians, pastors, and churches that affirm and proclaim the Fundamentals of the Faith. There has been a surge in the wave of faith.

The classical Christian school movement is part of just such a surge. It has borrowed from the weapons and ideals of historic, orthodox, Bible-believing Christianity. The Biblical doctrines that Machen fought for at old Princeton and later established at Westminster Theological Seminary form the heart of the theological outlook of classical Christian schools. Classical Christian schools are Bible-believing schools. The Scriptures are taught, affirmed, defended, and applied across the spectrum to all areas of school life and thought.

Almost all ideas are blended products from previous thought. Almost all applications of doctrines are processes that have been hammered out in controversies. Almost all movements are coalitions comprised of unlikely allies. The classical Christian education movement has borrowed from Dorothy Sayers, C. S. Lewis, Abraham Kuyper, J. Gresham Machen, and numerous others.

We have focused on three historical components of the modern classical Christian school movement. This account is an oversimplified version of what has happened. This movement also includes Anglicans, Lutherans, Orthodox, Catholic, Baptists, and various other Christians. The story is much more involved, for classical Christian education is a mighty river, and the many tributaries that flow into it are rivers themselves.

This chapter is longer than most of the chapters in this book. It is packed with history, names, book titles, and other details. Much of it may be unfamiliar to you. That in itself is yet another reason why your children need classical Christian education. We as parents have been so undereducated, so *mis*educated, and so uneducated that we don't even realize how much we don't know.

Assignment for Chapter 4

Read Hebrews 13:7. Consider the lives and conduct of those who have ministered to you in the past. Which of their traits do you find worth imitating? Think on, write down, and praise God for the many people he has used to impact your life through their faith and labors.

Scripture Memorization

Hebrews 13:7:

> Remember your leaders, those who spoke to you the word of God. Consider the outcome of their way of life, and imitate their faith.

Recommended Reading Assignments

Ben House, "Classical Christian Education: A Sampling of Some History" in *Punic Wars and Culture Wars: Christian Essays on History and Education* (Nacogdoches, TX: Covenant Media Press, 2008).

James Hilton, *Good-by, Mr. Chips* (New York: Little, Brown and Company, 1934).

C. S. Lewis, *Surprised by Joy: The Shape of My Early Life* (New York: HarperOne, 1955 [2017]).

J. Gresham Machen, *Christianity and Liberalism* (New York: Macmillan Company, 1923).

Abraham Kuyper, *Lectures on Calvinism* (Grand Rapids: Eerdmans, 1978).

CHAPTER FIVE

TRIVIUM PURSUIT

Mark Twain began *The Adventures of Huckleberry Finn* with Huck saying, "You don't know about me without you have read a book by the name of 'The Adventures of Tom Sawyer'; but that ain't no matter." Likewise, you don't know much about this chapter without you have read an essay by the name of "The Lost Tools of Learning" by Dorothy Sayers; but that ain't no matter. This chapter will cover the heartbeat and blood flow of classical Christian education. We will begin with Dorothy Sayers, the godmother of the modern classical Christian school movement.

Unlearning and Rediscovering

You met Dorothy Sayers (1893–1957) back in the previous chapter. She was a contemporary of and friend with C. S. Lewis. She attended Oxford University and was among the first women to receive a degree from there. In her day, she was a successful mystery writer, and she is still remembered for her Lord Peter Wimsey detective novels. She not only wrote popular fiction, but also serious theological works, including the book *The Mind of the Maker*, and she provided an eloquent translation of Dante's *Divine Comedy*. Also, her translation of *The Song of Roland* is still read and enjoyed by students in classical Christians schools. In the classical Christian world, however, she is best remembered for a paper wrote entitled "The Lost Tools of Learning," which she delivered at Oxford University in 1948. This was a brilliant discussion of what Ms. Sayers thought would be the ideal education. However, she doubted anyone would ever implement her proposal.

In her essay, she envisioned quite an array of amazing possibilities for the school of her dreams. But she made one major mistake in her essay: her pessimistic concern that no one would ever follow her suggestions has been proved totally wrong. Ideas have consequences, and essays have reprints. In her case, the essay was reprinted off and on in several places.

At a particular point in time in Idaho, a Reformed evangelical pastor remembered reading the essay during a time when he and some other men were talking about starting a Christian school. Distributing many copies of "The Lost Tools of Learning" to interested parents, he pitched the idea of erecting a classical Christian school. All agreed, and then they began asking each other, "What even is classical Christian education"?

The pastor is Douglas Wilson, and he has now written and contributed to quite a few books answering the question, "What even is classical Christian education"? The first book Wilson wrote on classical Christian education was *Rediscovering the Lost Tools of Learning.*[1] Sayers' essay is an appendix in that book—not just the heart.[2]

Step one, parents, is for you to read Dorothy Sayers' essay.[3] You will have either two response to the essay: either you will have a visceral response to it, dismissing it as a traditional impractical approach or you will have a visceral response to it, lamenting how modern progressive education has robbed you. Most of us are in a massive debriefing. (We say "most" because there are now a couple of generations who have not been robbed of their Christian education thanks to the resurgence of classical Christian education.) We have lots of unlearning to do. We have even more learning to do. We cannot perpetually plop ourselves into a recliner watching reality TV and meditating Facebook's wisdom and raise children who are godly readers, thinkers, and doers of the Holy Scriptures.

Here, we will recite only a few points from Sayers. First is the use of the Trivium—a threefold structure of instruction corresponding to the

---

[1] Douglas Wilson, *Rediscovering the Lost Tools of Learning: An Approach to Distinctively Christian Education* (Wheaton, IL: Crossway, 1991).

[2] Don't ask us how an appendix can pump blood.

[3] Good for you, we've included the essay as an appendix within THIS book.

natural, logical manner of receiving, retaining, and explaining knowledge. Modern, progressive education is besotted with the latest pedagogical trends and programs. It has a constant love affair with technological advancement. It is relentlessly loyal to "differentiated" instruction.[4] It lusts for the state-of-the-art. It is addicted to acronyms.

The Trivium, by contrast, is an educational innovation developed several millennia ago; it has been tested in the fiery forges of time. The educated people during Medieval Era (approximately 500 to 1500 A.D.), structured education around the Trivium. Before the Medieval Era, the ancient Romans and Greeks were educating in terms of the Trivium.

Okay, So What Is the "Trivium?"

The Trivium is not some snappy innovation or method that has popped up repeatedly throughout history. The reason why Greeks, Romans, and Jews used it is because it is the way education naturally works. It fits into the grooves of the mind and the way of all learning experiences. It can be said that teaching has been done according to the Trivium for as long as farming has been done using dirt to grow things. The Trivium is rooted not in a school curriculum, or in the mind of a philosopher, or in the handbook of a school; rather, it is rooted in the natural way God created us to learn. The Trivium is not honored and revered because it is old, but rather because it creates a better kind of student.

The three parts of the Trivium are as follows: Grammar, Logic, and Rhetoric.

First, memorize these words. Say them over and over. You will have then mastered the *grammar stage*.

Second, learn the definitions of these terms and see how they connect to each other to create meaning. Sayers' essay will give you the needed information for this (see the appendix below). When you see

---

[4] Regarding the pits of such differentiated instruction, see C. S. Lewis, "Democratic Education," originally published as "Notes on the Way," *Time and Tide* 29 (1944): 369–70.

how one part leads to and is built upon the other parts, then you have mastered the *logic stage*.

Finally, explain the Trivium to someone near you (perhaps, a person passing by you in a grocery store aisle or a neighbor sitting on his porch). You have now entered the realm of *rhetoric*.

In grammar school (or what we now call elementary school), we say, "Children, memorize the names of the first sixteen U. S. Presidents." (By the way, children in their elementary years have the best memory skills; furthermore, the key to grammar teaching and memorization is found in songs and chants.)

In junior high school, students begin the logic (or "dialectic") level. It is also called, by Sayers, the argumentative stage. Junior high kids—argumentative? That was a profound insight, Ms. Sayers. She sees that these often difficult traits of junior high kids are to be channeled toward more learning. Here, she recommends teaching formal logic as a course and implementing logical thinking. (They are going to argue, so why not equip them to argue intelligently?) So, the teacher is now having students debate and discuss President Washington's actions as President. What were his qualifications for office? What were the philosophical differences between Secretary of State Thomas Jefferson and Secretary of the Treasury Alexander Hamilton? How did other Presidents follow the precedents established by President Washington?

In high school, students are merging their grammar knowledge of things with an ever-growing logical understanding. They are increasingly ready for rhetoric—how to beautifully and persuasively communicate. So, they take a course called Rhetoric, with such hot, lively new authors as Aristotle, Cicero, Quintilian, and St. Augustine. But just as Logic is more than a course, so is Rhetoric. As a methodology, Rhetoric emphasizes learning how to interpret, analyze, and present material. This includes lots of writing, some debate, vast amounts of reading, a certain amount of answering objections, and verbalization of ideas.

The Goal of the Trivium: Learning How to Learn

Here it is important to keep in mind that these stages overlap and cannot exist without the other. Each stage is not entirely exclusive, but rather a matter of emphasis. Logic and rhetoric, for example, will rear its head during instruction within the first stage. Grammar never forsakes logic and rhetoric, and Logic undergirds the first and the third.

Here is Sayers' key point: True Education is teaching children how to learn. Her exact words were as follows: "For the sole true end of education is simply this: to teach men how to learn for themselves; and whatever instruction fails to do this is effort spent in vain."[5]

In other words, you could teach students the contents of a book—let's say *The Scarlet Letter* by Nathaniel Hawthorne. Your students learn the characters, plot, and symbolism of the book. Students ace the test; therefore, you believe are a good teacher. But what if the college professor assigns *A Hundred Years of Solitude*, *Things Fall Apart*, or a James Joyce novel? Could they *on their own* learn the characters, plot, and symbolism of the book? If not, perhaps they were never taught how to learn. If so, you have succeeded as an instructor.

Knowing the content of Hawthorne's book is useful, but such knowledge is incomplete. The needed skill is learning how to learn. Learning how to learn means learning to read and understand, how to think about a book, what questions to ask (yourself or the teacher), what ideas to consider, and how to break the code of the book or concept. In fact, over 50 years ago Jacob Klein of St. John's College in Annapolis, Maryland asserted that learning occurs in the classroom "not in the sense that students are being 'informed' about opinions and doctrines uttered in the books about events and facts mentioned in them, [or] about plots and stories presented and narrated." On the contrary, he argued "what is achieved is rather an expansion of the intellectual horizon, a fostering of understanding, a demolition of false assumptions."[6] This learning occurs chiefly through simple, yet critical, Socratic discussion.

---

[5] See Appendix 1.

[6] Jacob Klein, "Discussion as a Means of Teaching and Learning," *The College* (1971), 1. See Appendix 2.

Learning for Klein was not the ability to be informed, or to "download" information into the mind. Rather he envisioned learning as "the very effort to learn," following suit with the most ancient of pedagogues such as Plato and Socrates.

Learning How to Learn Is Work

Learning how to learn is a discipline. It is often incredibly challenging, yet it yields the results progressive schools long to exhibit. Classical Christian education could be called the Marine Corps of schooling. You don't send your children to a classical Christian school because it is easier. You don't send them there because you want them to graduate at age twelve. You don't send them there because you are afraid of government-funded public education. You send them to a classical Christian school to educate them—to teach them how to learn. This comes only through much sweat and tears (and perhaps some blood due to paper cuts from all the books we read).

Classical Christian schools are challenging. They involve homework. They stretch, pound, pulverize, recondition, and retrain the mind. In other words, classical Christian schools treat the mind like any average basketball coach treats the kids who show up to shoot hoops.

How would you respond if your child tried out for a high school basketball team whose coach said, "Alright, team, I am not going to make you run sprinting drills or lift weights because during the game we won't be running drills or lifting weights. Also we are going to share the ball so that no one gets more opportunity than anyone else. And we have lowered the goal to five feet and shortened the gym to twenty feet. And you don't have to dribble the ball; just carry it, that way you won't lose control of the ball. No one is allowed to take it away because each team member deserves to make at least two points."

NO to all that egalitarian nonsense in the field of athletics. No coach worth his salt will administer accommodations to players or modifications to the rules of the game for those players who are incapable of performing on the court or field. On the contrary, coaches scream themselves hoarse while pushing a bunch of out-of-shape kids to reach, strive, and achieve a level of play comparable to the professionals. If the standard for athletics is held high, why would we even consider lowering, dumbing-down, the standards for academics?[7]

You as a parent will be squeamish about the size and magnitude of what your children are learning. "Couldn't they just watch the movie instead of reading the book"? you might want to ask. "Do they really have to study Latin, take Rhetoric, and read Aristotle"? you might want to say. "They have so much homework," you might whine. "They are missing their childhood," you might think, failing to realize that classical education fosters the most imaginative childhood possible. Consider the following image we found on the internet:[8]

The image speaks for itself. Be prepared parents: if you come to understand what your child is receiving in a classical Christian school, you will find yourself becoming increasingly jealous of them.

Assignment for Chapter 5

Read and pray over Proverbs 1:1–7. What do these verses say about the goal and purposes education (*paideia*)? What does the sentence "The

---

[7] Even suggesting such is forbidden. Believe or not, there are schools that limit homework to 15–20 minutes per night, while the "subjects" of football, volleyball, and basketball receive a seemingly unlimited supply of "homework" time (A.K.A. before- and after-school practices, scrimmages, and competitions).

[8] You can find the original artist of this image on the Instagram profile Yo_Runner.

fear of the Lord is the beginning of knowledge" teach regarding any system of education that begins with ignoring God?

Scripture Memorization

Proverbs 1:2–7:

> To know wisdom and instruction, to understand words of insight, to receive instruction in wise dealing, in righteousness, justice, and equity; to give prudence to the simple, knowledge and discretion to the youth—Let the wise hear and increase in learning, and the one who understands obtain guidance, to understand a proverb and a saying, the words of the wise and their riddles. The fear of the LORD is the beginning of knowledge; fools despise wisdom and instruction.

Required Reading Assignments

Dorothy Sayers' essay "The Lost Tools of Learning" (See appendix 1 below).

Jacob Klein, "Discussion as a Means of Teaching and Learning" *The College* (1971): 1–2 (see appendix 2 below).

Recommended Reading Assignments

Louis Markos, *Passing the Torch: An Apology for Classical Christian Education* (Downers Grove, IL: InterVarsity Press, 2024).

Douglas Wilson, *Rediscovering the Lost Tools of Learning: An Approach to Distinctively Christian Education* (Wheaton, IL: Crossway, 1991).

Chapter Six

BOOKS, BOOKS, AND MORE BOOKS

Classics and Christian Formation

There goes the bell. It's time for class. With all the talk about classical Christian education, about the Trivium, and other topics, we must remember that school basically boils down to a few simple elements. You need a teacher, a book, and a student—preferably more than one student. Of course, desks, marker boards, lights, air conditioning, and (maybe) computers are helpful, but all those things are frosting on the cake.

We will focus the next several chapters on classes at the high school level primarily to focus on the end product—the capstone of a classical Christian education. In high school, or rhetoric school, we can better see the end results of classical Christian education. We can see students taking on the thoughts and patterns of a mature Christian disciple.

All high school students are, or are becoming, disciples. In elementary school, they are being disciplined or are being made into disciples (or both), but by the mid-teen years, they, themselves, are choosing, deciding, and determining the direction of their lives.

It is probable that several, possibly most, of the twelve apostles that were with Jesus were young men in their late teens (or at least early 20s). While there are late bloomers who do great things in their 50s, 60s, 70s, and so on (these individuals give Ben hope), it is amazing how many poets, scientists, philosophers, novelists, musicians, and others were on the road to great accomplishments early in life—as in, teenage years, late teenage years, and early 20s.

The goal for a graduating high school senior, from the parents' perspective, should be to go from one level of discipleship of Christ to another. Studies continually show that large numbers of church-raised kids abandon the faith in college. Before college is shunned or blamed, we must ask what these kids were like when they arrived at the university.

Remember that no school, no form of education, no academic experience can save the soul. Education can never result in spiritual regeneration (the new birth). But education can be a means of sanctification; that is, growth in grace.

Odysseys and Companions

Classical Christian education should and must result in spiritual training. Students will be reading Christian books that formed the world of Christendom. They must have the experience of seeing a volume of Augustine's *City of God* on the table and hearing the words *Tolle lege*, "take up and read." They need to know hell first hand, or at least first hand through reading Dante's *Inferno*. They need to know the terrible choice of Adam and Eve and of Satan's rebellion through Milton's *Paradise Lost*.[1]

And what shall we say of Narnia? Readings of Lewis' *The Chronicles of Narnia* instills adventure into younger children and provides older children with a vision of our world of modernity, of our calling to be kings and queens, and of good, godly rule. Lewis' friend J. R. R. Tolkien gave us another vision in his *The Hobbit*, *The Lord of the Rings*, and *The Silmarillion*—a vision of a kingdom on earth, of a home to defend, of the need for fellowship, and of the nature of evil.

The men and women of Jane Austen's novels show the propriety of good manners, decorum, and Christian culture. Some Austen characters show those virtues through their own lives, while others show them through exhibiting just the opposite behaviors.

And there is no end to the sanctifying models and examples from Shakespeare. Macbeth, the king in the play by the same name, should scare us all by his fall into sin. Hamlet, a prince, struggles with issues of revenge, justice, and procrastination. Henry V, emerging from the flaws of his years as Prince Hal, struggles with the role of a godly king. Petruchio models Christ as he seeks to change the shrewish nature of

---

[1] This is probably the only appropriate scenario where you can give your students hell.

Katarina into a godly nature in *The Taming of the Shrew*. Not to mention the petty grudge between the Montagues and Capulets which tragically results in (and is comedically resolved by) the death of their two beloved children.

We are all on a journey: kids in high school, graduates from high school, young people in college, adults, married couples, married couples with children, and people facing retirement years. Leo Tolstoy said that almost all stories hinge on taking a trip or a stranger coming to town. Students have much to learn about journeys. In Chaucer's *Canterbury Tales*, we learn that people, especially religious people, bring lots of baggage, lots of color and depth, and stories. Every story tells us something of either man's sinfulness or of man's inescapable stamp as God's image. Every story tells of something of a living faith God or the futility of life without God. And every story tells of something of why we are in this world.

Books and journeys: the two are inseparable. Huck and Jim, Dante and Virgil, Frodo and Sam, Eustace and Jill, and on and on it goes. This, of course, reminds us that it is not just books and journeys, but companions. "It is not good for man to be alone" (Gen 1:18). The call is always there for a friend, a brother, a friend closer than a brother, a husband, a wife, a soul mate, a fellow traveler. Robert Frost has said all this in his short poem, "The Pasture:"

> I'm going out to clean the pasture spring.
> I'll only stop to rake the leaves away,
> (And wait and watch the water clear, I may;)
> I sha'n't be gone long. You come too.
>
> I'm going out to fetch the little calf
> That's standing by its mother. It's so young
> It totters when she licks it with her tongue.
> I sha'n't be gone long. You come too.[2]

[2] Edward Connery Latham, ed., *The Poetry of Robert Frost*. (New York: Holt, Rinehard, and Winston, 1969), 1.

We Read *Books*

Speaking of poetry and Robert Frost … wait a minute. You are now either looking down, gazing out the window, or your eyes are glazed over. Perhaps all this wandering across the fields of literature is not convincing you of classical Christian education.

In classical Christian schools, we read books, big books, whole books—classics. In fact, when a student graduates, he or she can stack up the classics and serious books (excluding textbooks) and stand by this tower of books for a picture. The book stack usually equals or nearly equals the height of the student. (An admirable dream might be of a winning team of six-foot basketball players standing beside a six-foot stacks of books.)

But parents usually are not impressed with our reading lists. Moms and dads usually aren't anxious to fork over money simply to see their child with his or her nose in a thick volume of Charles Dickens all evening. The canon of Western literature, sad to say, is not a game changer.

We will be the first to admit that classical Christian education is bookish—heavily so; this is not a problem. We will be the first to admit that many of us in classical Christian schools never met a classic we didn't like or didn't want to teach; this is only natural. We will be the first to admit that the results of Gutenberg's printing press excites our minds more than the latest Microsoft, Apple, or other new technology; this is true. We will be the first to admit that teaching novels, plays, and poetry sure beats working for a living; also true.

If you are looking for the trendy, the latest, the newest, or the most high tech, perhaps classical Christian education really won't appeal to you. And this is definitely a problem, for we believe that classical Christian education is education. Full stop.

So, why is classical Christian education so behind the times? Why is it out of touch with the real world? Why is it so irrelevant to educational trends? Why are we obsessed with hefty classics?

Or, perhaps, a more precise question would be this: what happened to our part of the world that has forsaken the great books that once stood at the center of any understanding of "education"?

Why We Read

We teach books, big books, and classics because we want train and instruct poets and scientists. Preferably, we want to train and instruct poets with scientific understanding and scientists with poetic understanding. A scientist who can't appreciate Shakespeare's *A Midsummer Night's Dream* is severely lacking in his education; likewise, a poet who can't marvel at the physical and mathematical intricacies of creation probably shouldn't be reading poetry. One big reason is that poetry and science assists our understanding of Scripture—our understanding of the Triune God. In fact, the Bible presupposes our understanding of poetry and science. The Bible assumes that you have a working knowledge of agriculture, astronomy, arithmetic, and poetic meter.

By training poets, we do not mean people who sit at a desk or under a tree on a spring afternoon thinking up sentences that end in rhymes. Just ask Henry Wadsworth Longfellow or some currently popular and successful singer or songwriter. Good lyrics make big bucks. Words sell. Words convince. Words are created and words create. Churchill's speeches during World War II filled in a gap that the British military could not fill. The alphabet has more apps than your smart phone. The gospel is conveyed in words, as well as seen in deeds and acts of worship. Everyday life consists of an interchange of words. The world of business, the world of medicine, the world of economics, the world of art, and all worlds around us are conveyed in words. Words aren't merely markings on paper or icons on screens. Words are connectors between humans, across space and time, and beyond cultures. Words are pictures. Words are the most powerful technology man has.

So, why this bookish obsession? So that we can train poets, but what about scientists? There is a line of criticism that says that classical Christian education as a program is weak on math and science. People who envision their children being surgeons aren't usually won over by my joy over teaching future med students Herodotus and Herman Melville.

First witness: Albert Einstein. Einstein said that if you want a child to be a great physicist, let them read fairy tales. Einstein wasn't just having a bad hair day when he said this. (It should be noted that he had bad hair decades, not days.) He recognized that scientific advancement comes from being able to imagine, being able to create, and being able to do things others haven't done before. Hans Christian Anderson was able to imagine stories of magical things, hence fairy tales. Mark Twain was able to imagine a rogue and rowdy white kid who rides a raft down the Mississippi with a runaway slave. C. S. Lewis was able to imagine a parallel world entered through a wardrobe. Dante imagined a journey through Hell, Purgatory, and Heaven. Likewise, Albert Einstein was able to imagine some formulas and applications of science.

It all gets back to the ability to think. It all gets back to Dorothy Sayers' call for teaching children how to think. It all gets back to the Trivium. You fill in the blanks in the grammar of learning, connect the dots in the logic of learning, and surmise that perhaps E equals MC squared in the rhetoric of learning.

To have an education built around the Trivium and to have an education that is weak in math and science is a contradiction. Let's review and apply the Trivium again. Note also, that each new subject—such as chemistry, biology, or physics—involves an implementation of the Trivium.

The Grammar Stage: the essential facts of the subject. Numbers, scientific data, definitions, terminology.

The Logic Stage: connections between the facts. Learning how number processes work, learning the connections between scientific facts, learning the effects of mixing chemical elements, and so on.

The Rhetoric Stage: at this stage, the student is experimenting, explaining, theorizing, comparing and contrasting, and mastering the subjects.

Okay, we have covered quite a bit here. We have emphasized literature and reading, but have hopefully made the case for classical Christian education being effective in the sciences and math. Straying off the subject, which is really thinking about where the subject leads us, is a vital part of education.

Assignment for Chapter 6

Read 2 Timothy 4:13. Pray over the passage and consider the implications regarding how highly Paul valued his reading materials.

Scripture Memorization

1 Timothy 4:13:

> Until I come, devote yourself to the public reading of Scripture, to exhortation, to teaching.[3]

Recommended Reading Assignments

C. S. Lewis, "On the Reading of Old Books" in *Essay Collection and Other Short Pieces* (New York: HarperCollins, 2000).

C. S. Lewis, *An Experiment in Criticism* (Cambridge: Cambridge University Press, 1961).

Louis Markos, *Myth Made Fact: Reading Greek and Roman Mythology through Christian Eyes* (Camp Hill, PA: Classical Academic Press, 2015).

Louise Cowan and Os Guinness, editors. *An Invitation to the Classics: A Guide to Books You've Always Wanted to Read* (Grand Rapids: Baker, 2006) .

---

[3] God created language, and he loves it when his people *read*.

CHAPTER SEVEN

VIRTUOUS (AND NOT-SO-VIRTUOUS) PAGANS

We have problems with most (not all) government-run, secular humanist, tax-payer financed public school systems. We know that there are good things that public schools do, and we have known many good and dedicated teachers in the system. Again, we have both taught in the public school sector, and at the time of this books publication Colton teaches for a public school. In spite of the many failures, complaints, and problems in the vast network of public education, there are many successes.

Nonetheless, we have problems with "those schools." In particular, we have one big problem: most don't read enough bad books. They don't teach enough about paganism. There is not enough violence, sexual immorality, and evil in the literature. In other words, they don't teach books that reflect a biblical assessment of the world.

The history of the world and the recurring themes of literature are stories of war, murder, idolatry, avarice, ambition, unrestrained cruelty, mayhem, crime, vandalism, sexual immorality and religious hypocrisy. For a short proof-text of that sentence, read the book of Judges. The book of Judges and its sixty five other companion volumes are themselves either ignored or minimized in public schools, which is another glaring problem.

"Let Them at Least Have Heard of Brave Knights"

Parents with small children, don't panic. We are not talking about teaching vivid Homeric descriptions of spear wounds from the Trojan War, atrocities from the First and Second World Wars, or the disgusting details of the culture wars of our times to kindergarteners and really young children. The violence of "Goldilocks and the Three Bears," "Little Red Riding Hood," and "The Three Little Pigs" are plenty for them to deal with. Our very young children can learn to read and imagine a world of fire-breathing dragons that get punctured by knights in shining armor. We are focusing on the high school years. Consider C. S. Lewis' words:

> Those who say that children must not be frightened may mean two things. They may mean (1) that we must not do anything likely to give the child those haunting, disabling, pathological fears against which ordinary courage is helpless: in fact, phobias. His mind must, if possible, be kept clear of things he can't bear to think of. Or they may mean (2) that we must try to keep out of his mind the knowledge that he is born into a world of death, violence, wounds, adventure, heroism and cowardice, good and evil. If they mean the first I agree with them: but not if they mean the second. The second would indeed be to give children a false impression and feed them on escapism in the bad sense. There is something ludicrous in the idea of so educating a generation which is born to the … atomic bomb. Since it is so likely that they will meet cruel enemies, let them at least have heard of brave knights and heroic courage. Otherwise you are making their destiny not brighter but darker.[1]

To the question about whether there is enough violence and evil in the world, the answer is "No." There is too much violence and evil in the world. That is why God has been on a spiritual and physical quest to kill, destroy, and remove (or, in some cases, convert) every dragon, demonic being, tyrant, ogre, troll, renegade, vandal, cannibal, murderer, thief, hypocrite, and evil devising person.

God's Law, revealed in both the Scriptures and in the heart of man, has been given as a great holding action, designed to restrain, punish, and redirect huge swaths of wicked behavior. God's greatest offensive against all the wickedness of man was in sending His Son, who surprisingly first appeared as a baby in a manger, who then went to the cross to defeat sin, Satan, and death. God also established the Church as

---

[1] C. S. Lewis, *Of Other Worlds: Essays and Stories* (San Diego: Harvest Books, 2002), 31.

an offensive weapon, through the empowering work of the Holy Spirit that will push the enemies of God all the way back to the gates of Hell.

Jesus did not come to merely elevate the religious impulses of His times. He did not come to do some minor home improvements on His Father's world. He did not come here to give us some extra tutoring to bring our low B- to an A+.

Christ came to save sinners. Christ came into a world that was cruel, God-hating, self-devouring, and wicked to the core. Christ came to people who were deformed by sin, grotesque in heart and soul, and corrupted. The gospel is not pretty. It is life-support being hooked up and pumping blood into dead, rotting corpses. Again, the gospel isn't pretty, but the results are beautiful. The ugliness of sin and the horrible nature of sinners is the result of the perversion of what we were supposed to be. Our hearts yearn for a God-centered world, and yet they still rebel against it. We have, almost as it were, a distant memory of a garden, a place that was far better than this, a life that would be different from this one. We are the Noldor living in the Third Age of Middle Earth, remembering the beatific lands of Valinor and longing yet again to traverse the Western Sea.[2]

We still try to do gardening in a dessert. We grow thorns and thistles and call them fruit and vegetables. We walk, stumble actually, blind and deaf, through the darkened world, while boasting of what we vainly call beauty in sight and sound. We carve idols out of wood or mass produce them with plastic and call them our gods and saviors.

Because man is made in the image of God, he is capable of doing great things. Because man is fallen into sin, the great things he does often are twisted, warped, and fashioned into instruments of hell. The beauty of man's image bearing and the ugliness of man's sin can be seen in all cultures at all times.

Pagans Paving the Path

Jesus Christ came into a world of three rich intersecting cultures. One was the Hebrew culture. It was a culture primarily of one book: the

---

[2] See J. R. R. Tolkien, *The Silmarillion*, Christopher Tolkien, ed. (New York: HarperCollins, 2014).

Tanakh, otherwise known as the Old Testament.[3] It had a big advantage over the other two cultures because God spoke to the prophets and gave His Law to them. That part was good. However, those who received the truth rebelled against it, distorted and ignored it, and often acted worse than those who received no revelation.

Another dominant culture of Jesus' time was the Greek culture. We often speak of the post-Alexander the Great world as the Hellenistic world (and the time as the Hellenistic Age). Greek culture was the idea factory of the ancient world. Greeks whipped out epic poems, tragic and comic dramas, lyric poetry, histories, biographies, philosophies, political treatises, scientific research papers, literary criticism, logic and rhetoric texts, and they still had time to strip to the buff and run races and wrestle for laurel leaves every four years in the shadow of incredible architectural wonders, such as Corinthian and Doric columns.

The Greek world of thought and action was like Hollywood and Broadway, Harvard and Yale, Wall Street and main street, Disneyworld and the Internet all wrapped up in togas and largely located in the tree-lined groves of Academe, just outside of Athens.

The New Testament includes writings written as missiles[4] making direct hits on aspects of Greek thought and as bulldozers designed for clearing away Greek rubble. But after the bombing and the clearing, there were broken Greek things that have been salvaged and used by Christians and Western Civilization. The New Testament itself, we must remember, did not come down the ages to us through Hebrew or King James English. It was written in Greek and in the Greco-Roman milieu under Rome's domination. God used the Greek language in part to provide a mechanism for telling people about Jesus.[5]

Long before the Greek-written inspired texts of the Gospels and Epistles appeared, God gave a whole host of Greeks with speaking,

---

[3] "Tanakh" is an acronym referring to the threefold division of the Hebrew Scriptures: the Torah (Pentateuch), Nevi'im (Prophets), and Ketuvim (Writings).

[4] Epistles as Missiles—a phrase worth thinking about and using later.

[5] See Augustine, *On Christian Teaching*, 2.15.22. Cf. Colton Moore, "Graeca Veritas: Saint Augustine's Historical and Theological Rationale for the Septuagint as Authoritative Scripture" in Mariusz Szram and Marcim Wysocki, eds., *Studia Patristica CIII: The Bible in the Patristic Period* (Peeters: Leuven, 2021), 158–62.

poetic, writing, and thinking skills. There were probably vast libraries or lots of bards for hire who could access the materials faster than a Dewey Decimal driven librarian or a Google link.

Vast numbers of manuscripts were lost or broken up. Still, a large number of books remain. We call them the Greek classics. The ancient and revered names of Homer, Hesiod, Aeschylus, Sophocles, Euripides, Herodotus, Thucydides, Socrates, Plato, and Aristotle are sounded forth.

If you recognize the names, you deserve a pat on the back. If you can associate a book, play, or idea with each name, you deserve an ice cream cone. If you have read those authors and can comment on their writings, you likely either lived in the 1800s (or before) or you have had exposure to a classical school.

Athenians, Take Note: Greek Philosophy is a Dead End Street

The key to understanding Greek literary works is to see them as inverted, warped Gospel accounts, man-centered law, humanistic poetry, and godless prophecies. In other words, the Greek literary works include the same categories as our Bible, and the Greek writings can stand alongside our Old and New Testaments. Oh, we should add this, there is one major difference: the Greeks got it wrong—or at least much of it wrong.

Greek stories are inverted gospel stories. They are the "good news of salvation" to a world without the true God. The good news of the Greeks is basically that there is no good news. No one ever walked the aisle, accepted Zeus in his heart, which resulted in living a better life. No one ever died to be with Zeus on Mount Olympus. The Greeks, as noted by Greek literary scholar Paul of Tarsus, realized that "in Him (the true God) we live and move and have our being." The Greeks grasped that "we are also His offspring." And he noted that Greeks and others would "seek the Lord, in the hope that they might grope for Him and find Him, though He is not far from each one of us." (All these insights from Paul are found in his lectures series titled "Athenians, Take Note: Greek Philosophy is a Dead End Street," commonly known as Acts 17.)

It has often been said or read that all philosophy is but footnotes to Plato. We could trace many novels, stories, plays, and movies back to the stories and ideas found in Homer and the Greek dramatists. There is no escaping the pervasive impact of ancient Greek culture, and there is no evading the perverted remnants of Greek thought and life. You could run a marathon (a Greek word, μαραθών) every day in your Nikes ("Nike" comes from νίκη, meaning "victory") and still not come reach the exit door to Greek influences in our world.

Whether the motivation is "know your enemy," "know your neighbor," or "know your history and culture," we simply cannot get from here to there without going through Athens.

Rather than write a whole book at this point on Greek culture or force you into a whole year of class studying the influence of the Greeks, we limit ourselves to one story, and only a few fragments of that. Which story? Maybe, we could discuss *The Bacchae* by Euripides. It is a powerful example of a warped Christmas story. Maybe, we could discuss *Antigone* by Aeschylus. All stories of right opposing might echo that story, as well as all stories about a woman exhibiting strength and determination while under threat.

Then there is the *Odyssey*. It is the story of journeys—the journey of all journeys—and it is the story about stories. It is about the mind, growing up, taking on responsibilities, true love, mortality, the quest of the mind, and the adventures of life. Homer's *Odyssey* is the story of man's need to learn what matters, whether it is Odysseus himself doing the learning, or his son Telemachus. But let us go back a bit to the prior epic, the story that preceded Odysseus' ten year journey.

Let us step onto the plains of Troy, outside the high walls of that city, ten years in the great war incited over a woman. Now, two great warriors are locked in a battle; two great warriors fighting, who are on the same side:

> Rage—Goddess, sing the rage of Peleus' son Achilles,
> murderous, doomed, that cost the Achaeans countless losses,
> hurling down to the House of Death so many sturdy souls,
> great fighters' souls, but made their bodies carrion,
> feasts for the dogs and birds,

> and the will of Zeus was moving toward its end.
> Begin, Muse, when the two first broke and clashed,
> Agamemnon lord of men and brilliant Achilles. (*Iliad*, 1–8)[6]

Certainly, we would hope that those opening lines would be more than a bait luring you to this book, but rather a hook securing you into this epic. But a few preliminaries before we take up arms on the plains of Troy.

First, a confession. Ben and Colton were not educated in Greek literature. We had a Trivial Pursuit knowledge, as in "Who wrote the *Iliad*"? When I (Ben) first read it (long after college and over 15 years of teaching), I was pleased with myself more than I was with either Homer.

I (Ben, again—yes, it's confusing when one author who co-authors a book breaks into the first-person singular. Sorry.) thought the book consisted of an incredible amount of war, fighting, and puncturing of entrails. Quite frankly, I preferred the histories of the American Civil War Between the States or World War II over this poetic account of the Trojan War. Besides, Homer made a major blunder. In the *Iliad*, he never talked about the Trojan Horse, nor did he describe Achilles' death by an arrow to his heel.

"This is a great classic," I said aloud to my classes, but secretly I wondered what was so great about it. It was somewhere around my third reading, somewhere in the midst of hearing some good teachers, who were literary scholars, praise the book, somewhere in a literary conversion (while in my mid-forties) that I began realizing the depth, organization, beauty, and soul-wrenching nature of the poem. My feeling the spear wounds, my weeping over the strewn bodies of both Achaeans and Trojans, and my pain and joy over the story only came and now continues after repeated readings.

In my earlier readings, I thought Achilles was an overly emotional, selfish, whining super-soldier, who sulked in his tent during most of the book. "Okay, Achilles, things didn't go your way. Someone took your

---

[6] Homer, *Iliad*, Robert Fagles, trans. (New York: Penguin, 1996).

girlfriend. So what"? Wasn't the country song "Tennessee Waltz,"[7] as well as a thousand other stories and songs about love lost, equal to the *Iliad*? Besides, Achilles got his girl back.

Then it began to become clear: Achilles didn't just lose a girlfriend or undergo some humiliation in front of the other military officers. He lost the opportunity and right he had to be god. Not just god, but God, or at least in Greek terms, the chief god and deity over the other Greek gods. Achilles and Jesus could have had a long conversation. Everything that worked to accomplish Jesus' mission, despite Satan's attempts to thwart his mission, worked the other way in Achilles' life. Achilles, in short, was a failed Jesus figure.

Achilles was a child of prophecy, like Jesus. He should have been divine, like Jesus. Immortal, like Jesus. Lord of lords and King of Kings, like Jesus. His mother, Thetis, was a beautiful goddess (and a great swimmer). Any guy would want to marry Thetis. Of course, Zeus, the BMOO (Big Man on Olympus) was interested. After all, she was female and really cute. His brother Poseidon, ruler over the seas, was also interested. But both guys kept their distance.

It was prophesied that the son of Thetis would be greater than the father. In the Greek world, the offspring of a deity and a human was a mortal. The offspring of two deities would be an immortal deity. Zeus Junior would have bested his daddy, just as Zeus bested his own father, Cronus. Likewise, Poseidon II would have taken over his dad's realm. The child of Thetis would rule Mount Olympus and the other gods or rule the oceans. The child of Thetis would excel his father. So, Zeus and Poseidon, in a rare case of controlling their own sexual appetites, protected their rule and pushed Thetis into marriage with a mortal named Peleus. Peleus really seemed to be a nice guy, a decent father, and, likely, a good warrior, but he was mortal. He was born, he lived, and he died. So would his son Achilles.

Achilles was a super-warrior. Imagine all the current super-heroes, such as Ironman, Spider Man, the Incredible Hulk, and others. Achilles could have taken them all on and won.

---

[7] "And while they were dancing, my friend stole my sweetheart from me."

Here comes the next conversation between Jesus and Achilles. Both faced early deaths. Mortality is, perhaps, the greatest issue, conflict, threat, and sobering aspect of life in this world. There would only be life, as in salvation, if Jesus died. Jesus had to die in order for us to live. The Cross would be the defining woodwork in Jesus' mission. Achilles also had to die if he were to accomplish anything and if he were to achieve the only salvation possible for him and his world. But what Achilles would accomplish with his death was a hollow victory.

Eternal life in the Homeric world was glory and honor—the ever-ringing praise of the plebs (well, undying insofar as humans keep praising a Greek hero). People would sing the glory of Achilles and enjoy the fruits of victory over Troy for generations to come. But to accomplish that, Achilles had to die.

Sacrifice is a pretty big concept. Try thinking about American history and our heritage of liberty without the idea of sacrifice involved. Remove sacrifice from the Bible and all that is left is paper pulp and ink.

Achilles had to give up his life, his future, the pleasantries of the family farm back in Greece, watching his own boys play in the surf of the Aegean Sea, and everyday pleasures of life—all just so poets would sing of him. So that young boys would aspire to his muscles and military exploits. So that monuments, streets, and military bases would be named for him.

But Achilles would be dead. Deity denied. Mortality certain. Destiny unavoidable. Death to death, ashes to ashes, without hope of resurrection. Yet, Achilles would receive honor *in extremis*. That's at least a plus, right? Wrong.

The Providence of the Triune God rescues us from the despair of the Greek Fates. God's covenant in Christ gives a greater promise than Greek despair. Jesus' victory over sin and death is greater than Achilles' victory over Troy. When Achilles' died, the object of his hope deceived him. When Jesus died, he became the object of our hope so that when we die we do not despair in the House of Death but ever sing the praises of him who made a way into eternal life.

Homer's epic, when carefully read and cultivated, can give us a greater sense of the sheer height, depth, and beauty of the true gospel. Homer's *Iliad* emotionally and intellectually fills the heart, but breaks it. The sorrow and despair it brings would have no limit were it not for the *Iliad*'s counterpoint, the gospel of Jesus Christ.

Alright, that's a lot of introduction. Class begins in just a few minutes. Won't you join us and sit in on a few classes? We'll provide lunch.

Assignment for Chapter 7

Read Acts 17:16–34. Carefully note Paul's use of pagan sources in verse 28. The whole passage is an interaction of the New Testament message to the Greek mindset. It is rich in lessons for defending the faith, witnessing to the lost, and using unbelievers' background to explain the gospel. What could this passage teach us about education for our children?

Scripture Memorization

Acts 17:26–28:

> And he made from one man every nation of mankind to live on all the face of the earth, having determined allotted periods and the boundaries of their dwelling place, that they should seek God, and perhaps feel their way toward him and find him. Yet he is actually not far from each one of us, for "In him we live and move and have our being"; as even some of your own poets have said, "For we are indeed his offspring."

Recommended Reading Assignments

Peter Leithart, *Heroes of the City of Man: A Christian Guide to Select Ancient Literature* (Moscow, ID: Canon Press, 1999).

Louis Markos, *From Achilles to Christ: Why Christians Should Read the Pagan Classics* (Downers Grove, IL: IVP Academic, 2007).

Edith Hamilton, *Mythology: Timeless Tales of Gods and Heroes* (New York: Little Brown & Company, 1942).

PART 2

COME AND TAKE A TOUR

(LUNCH PROVIDED)

CHAPTER EIGHT

1ST PERIOD: THE RHETORIC OF LOGIC AND THE LOGIC OF RHETORIC

We hoped you liked literature class. Hopefully, you are at least more curious about classical literature and more open to your children being guided along through the labyrinth of Greek culture with the light of Scripture providing the interpretation.

On now to first period: Logic and Rhetoric. We'll spend half our time in Logic and the other half just across the hallway in Rhetoric. You're in for a treat.

Logic and Rhetoric Compared

One of the founding fathers of formal Logic and Rhetoric was Aristotle.[1] He begins his book *Rhetoric* with these words:

> Rhetoric is the counterpart (or antistrophe) of Dialectic [Logic]. Both alike are concerned with such things as come, more or less, within the general ken of all men and belong to no definite science. Accordingly, all men make use, more or less, of both; for to a certain extent all men attempt to discuss statements and to maintain them, to defend themselves and to attack others. (*Rhet.* 1.1)

In the context of a classical Christian education, Rhetoric is a class that students take after they have taken Logic class. Both subjects deal with matters that affect all people in all areas. We think and speak all the time, about a host of subjects and in everyday life. We talk about

---

[1] Andrew Kern has recently argued that Aristotle learned his logic and rhetoric from Homer's epic poem. See Colton's podcast, the *Christ & Classics Podcast*, to hear Kern's argument. "Homer the Pedagogue", *Christ & Classics Podcast*, 24 April 2024, https://www.youtube.com/watch?v=DcTq8UdTZ9M.

family conflicts, favorite sports teams, what to eat for dinner, Newton's three laws of motion, which Bible-reading plan is best, which job to take, which house in which to live, whom to marry, how to raise children, where to send those children for school (like this book), and so forth. In all such areas, we necessarily employ logic and rhetoric.

Everyone thinks through a matter and then states what they are thinking. If someone disagrees, then they naturally defend what they say. To do this well is to employ logic and rhetoric.

The words logic and rhetoric were used earlier in this work to describe stages of learning. Let's review. It all starts with the Trivium: Grammar, Logic, and Rhetoric. The Grammar stage is, more or less, Kindergarten through 5th grade; this stage emphasizes the "grammar" of all things: the building blocks and basic facts of common knowledge. The Logic stage comes next, typically in the 6th–8th grades. It is the stage where students make connections of facts and begin questioning more intently the reasons of existence. The Rhetoric stage takes place at the high school level. Here the student is mastering reading, analyzing, explaining, presenting, and debating information.

Bear in mind that each stage is not mutually exclusive. Each phase will contain aspects of the others. It is only a matter of emphasis within each stage. The words Logic and Rhetoric also refer to specific classes that students take in classical Christian schools.

A course on formal Logic can be taken with profit at any time in secondary school, but it is best taught at the logic stage. It is thought that teaching Logic at this stage of life best fit's the mental development of the student. Is it any wonder why middle school pre-teens are experts in the art of arguing? Formal logic positively channels such ferocious energy!

Rhetoric courses take place in high school. Children are using rhetoric from infancy and are honing rhetorical skills all through school, but are best able to understand and improve these skills in the Rhetoric stage, or high school stage, of learning. While all upper level courses should be using the tools of rhetoric, the Rhetoric class itself focuses on how to define, understand, use, and improve rhetorical skills. (We'll lead you quietly to the back of the classroom; it looks like the instructor has just begun the lesson!)

First, Logic

Logic teachers don't actually begin their classes by saying, "All right, kids, listen closely and I'm going to tell you how to beat your parents in arguments." As parents, you may find that your classically-trained children are answering you by citing informal fallacies after they have begun taking a course in logic.

"Dad, that's an *ad baculum* fallacy."

"Mom, not only are you using a *Post hoc ergo propter hoc*, but you are also denying the antecedent."

Be calm. You are still in charge and, logically, you are on solid grounds to punish if the Algebra grade doesn't come up. Kids learning how to argue effectively is not an open door to disrespect and disobedience. Kids will attempt to use logic to their own advantage.

So should we avoid teaching it? No. Kids use grammar, the laws of science, and literacy to their own advantage as well. All of us are prone to use the tools of learning in ways that are misleading and sinful. If you teach someone to read, you have opened the door to them reading and embracing radical politics, immoral lifestyles, and soul-destroying heresies. Learning is not salvation. Alternatively, ignorance does not protect us from sin. All things must be sanctified and purified by faith and prayer. This includes formal Logic studies.

Logic is the study of thinking skills. The use of logic does not begin when someone enrolls in logic class in eighth grade. It is present when the infant realizes that screaming louder gets results. The baby calculates the effectiveness of a hypothetical syllogism:[2]

1. "If I whimper at this lower level, then my needs are met within minutes.
2. But if I scream and turn red in the face at this higher level, then relief appears in seconds.
3. Therefore …"

[2] A syllogism is a manner of reasoning where a single conclusion follows from two assumed premises. Hypothetical syllogisms follow the pattern of "If …, then …, therefore …"

Logic is not a source of truth for any system. A truth statement, such as this sentence, is neither logical or illogical. It is a premise that one accepts or denies for reasons generally unrelated to the laws of logic. No one can logically say, "My argument is right because it is logical and yours is wrong because it is not."

A Christian can be illogical and still correct. For example, our buddy might argue, "Jesus is the Son of God because we asked him to help us win the church softball league, and we did."

Bless our buddy's heart.

His conclusion ("Jesus is the Son of God") is correct, but his reasoning is illogical. Certainly, Jesus is the Son of God. Our buddy and the other good ole boys did ask Jesus to help them win the softball game, which they did win. But Jesus is not the Son of God *because* they asked him to help them. The proof of the proposition does not logically follow.

Our buddy committed the fallacy of *affirming the consequent* (if you want to know how it is termed in the logic book). *Affirming the consequent* is when you assert the "if" clause on the basis of the "then" clause in an "if-then" statement. It works like this:

1. <u>If</u> Jesus is the Son of God, <u>then</u> we will win the softball game.
2. We win the softball game.
3. <u>Therefore</u>, Jesus is the Son of God.

In technical logic "code" the fallacy of *affirming the consequent* looks like this:

1. <u>If</u> P, <u>then</u> Q.
2. Q.
3. <u>Therefore</u>, P.

Conclusions (main points and ideas) are supported by premises (reasons). The "if" clause in the "if-then" statement above is a premise; the "then" clause is the conclusion. The problem with *affirming the consequent* is that it is logically backwards. It turns the conclusion into the premise, and the premise into the conclusion. Our victory in the softball game isn't necessarily due to Jesus being the Son of God.

Let's look at another example. An unbeliever says, "The horrendous and wicked atrocities that happen in this world prove there is no perfectly good, all loving God who rules the world." What he is saying, in terms of a logical syllogism, is this:

1. If horrible and evil things happen, then a wise, loving God doesn't exist.
2. Horrible and evil things happen.
3. Therefore, there is no God.

Unlike the example above, which reverses the premise and conclusion, this argument is logically sound. It uses a logical form called *modus ponens*, which is structured in this way:

If P, then Q.
P.
Therefore, Q.

Though this argument is valid (logical), its validity (logic) does not prove its truthfulness. Good Christians can be illogical and unbelievers can be logical. *Logic does not prove an argument's truthfulness any more than grammar does.*

Math doesn't work that way either. There are ten apples. I eat two of them. How many do I have left? The formula 10 – 2 = 8 does not actually mean that I truly have any apples.

But let's run the grammar point by and look at it: a Christian from the rural south may say, "They ain't no way the Bible is wrong because God done wrote it Hisself." But an unbeliever says, "There is no way the Bible can be trusted because it was written by mortal men living long ago."

The grammar teacher gives an A+ to the unbeliever and an F to the Christian. But whose statement is true?

See our point?

Math, grammar, literacy, and logic are tools. So are hammers. As tools, they are God-given. We can change the rules of basketball. Some years back, there was no three-point line. Now there is a line on the basketball court. Also, grammar rules are subject to change through usage and agreed-upon conventions. Yes, you can split an infinitive, and you can end a sentence with a preposition. Double negatives can be used for emphasis. However, you cannot so change grammar that "I am married" means, "I am single, so let's go have lunch."

Logic can be used by unbelievers. We don't reject the unbelievers' logic; rather, we reject their premises (reasons) or statements (conclusions supported by premises). Unbelievers breath the air God created, walk on the earth he made, and use their God-given minds to construct arguments against Him. The Christian reaction to every broken and misused thing in God's world is not to escape from the world, but to "take every thought captive" (2 Corinthians 10:5) and bring the blessings of redemption to the world. We are to take our salvation to our minds and thought processes and from there to all areas of life. An unbeliever can and will misuse every mental process. Believers are to be salt and light in every corrupt and dark area of the world, and that commission includes the thought processes.

Logic trains the mind. Some terms and exercises in a logic class and logic books rarely appear in life experiences outside of the class itself. This includes phrases such as *modus ponens*, *modus tollens*, *affirming the consequent*, *denying the antecedent*, *ipse dixit*, *undistributed middle*, and so on. Specific, technical jargon appears in every class. Names in a literary work and problems in higher math also don't have a lot of action outside of the academic disciplines.

Then what's the point of knowing such highfalutin terms?

If you just asked that question, you have a long way to go in education—you have shown too many of your cards. You may have just indicated that you might be one of those darned utilitarians that have lamentably infiltrated our educational systems and have ruined the minds and hearts of millions of students in America.

Inside the classroom, understanding such impractical phrases and concepts are what constitute learning—mind stretching, concept building, and intellectual gymnastics. Understanding how to learn *to the nth*, which includes memorizing technical definitions, is education.

(Whenever you ask the question "when will I ever *use* that?" of any facet of education, there's a 99.9% chance you are a dirty utilitarian. "When will I ever use that" is a bad—terribly bad—question. Imagine how foolish it would be if a student athlete asked his coach that question about lifting weights, sprints, bleacher runs, push-ups, sit ups: "Coach, we'll *never* have to do squats on the basketball courts. Therefore, why do I have to do them?" We'll let your imagination run wild with how a good coach might respond. The tools of learning are like athletic conditioning: once you learn how to use them, your thinking and learning muscles "grow," influencing and shaping every aspect of your life. So, when will we ever use logic? *Every single day*.)

Christian education is designed to create Christian culture—that is, logical Christian ways of thinking, acting, living, ministering, and cultivating all of God's gifts. Christians must to produce logical thinkers. We must to produce the scientific and literary minds, the creators and inventors, the managers and the electricians alike, and so on. Logic class takes us one significant step along that path.

Next, Rhetoric

Neither Logic nor Rhetoric teaches us what to think. Rather, they teach us how to think or how to express what we think. "How" is the heartbeat of a classical education. And as we think about the "How," we must keep a doctrinal foundation in focus; this will provide the formative concepts in our children's beliefs. The school, let us remember, supplements faith and doctrine alongside the church and family.

Our faith beliefs are always in need of being recalled, applied, defended, and exported. Second Timothy 3:16 tells us that "All Scripture is given by the inspiration of God and is profitable for doctrine (teaching), for reproof, for correction, and for instruction in righteousness." Aristotle says, "all men attempt to discuss statements and to maintain them, to defend themselves and to attack others" (*Rhet.* 1.1).[3]

Paul and Aristotle could have been team-teaching at this point. Aristotle says that all men discuss statements and maintain them. Paul

---

[3] All translations of Aristotle's Rhetoric are taken from Aristotle, *The Rhetoric and Poetics of Aristotle*, Edward P. J. Corbett, trans. (New York: The Modern Library, 1984).

says that Scripture provides the framework for those statements and that we are to use Scripture for a particular kind of instruction—specifically, teaching righteous, godly living. Aristotle says that men defend statements, and Paul says, "Very true, Aristotle; so Christian, give a defense of your beliefs by correcting and reproving according to Holy Scripture." Aristotle then says that all men attempt to attack others. Paul lessens the abrasiveness of this by pointing out that the goal of this attack is correction.

All of these components, whether it is Aristotle's list (discussing, maintaining, defending, or attacking statements) or Paul's list (teaching, reproving, correcting, or instructing) involve communication. In order to accomplish the goals, that communication must be effective. (We could digress on the extent to which ineffective communication is really communication, but we would be ineffectively communicating what we aim to communicate here.)

Rhetoric has been defined as the art of persuasion. Aristotle defines it as finding the best possible means of persuasion. Rhetoric involves speaking, writing, and thinking in such a way as to persuade or be persuaded toward certain things and to resist persuasion toward other matters.

In classical education, Rhetoric is a formal class that involves talking in front of others; it is a class that includes public speaking. Rhetoric entails, as Cicero aptly stated, the theory, imitation, and practice of public oratory. Rhetoric class helps students overcome fear of speaking in front of an audience; it improves students' ability to enunciate words, speak loudly enough to be heard, make eye contact with the audience, and project self-confidence.

But these are the by-products of rhetoric class. Rhetoric class can also be compared to a writing class. Students write persuasive, descriptive, comparison-contrast, and other types of essays. Students practice re-writing, editing, and shaping up prose. And not just prose, students can focus on reading and writing poetry as well.

Research skills are also used. Students learn to find the best sources, to buttress an argument with good quotes, and to format, footnote, and attribute their research. The writing of the old tried and true "five paragraph essay" is practiced, honed, and, improved upon by young budding essayists.

But even these are by-products of rhetoric class. Rhetoric class is an extension of classical studies and literary readings. Students in Rhetoric class read the old dead Greek and Roman authors. Central to Rhetoric in classical Christian schools is the reading of Aristotle's *Rhetoric*, Cicero's *Rhetorica ad Herrenium*, and Quintilian's multiple volumes on rhetoric. Along with that, students should read Augustine's *De Doctrina Christiana* (*On Christian Teaching*), which is his Christian application of the tools of rhetoric.

Rhetoric students might watch lawyers defending their clients, a pastor expounding a text of Scripture, a professor in a college presenting a lecture, two political opponents debating a law, an advertisement seeking to sell toothpaste, or an actor delivering the defining speech in a play or movie. On that last point, students can profit from watching Kenneth Branagh's rendition of Henry V's "St. Crispin's Day" speech from the cinematic version of Shakespeare's play *Henry V*.

We live in, move, and have our being in a world of rhetoric. When asked the question "What is the most important speech you will ever give," male students usually revert to the safe sounding religious answer, "Witnessing to someone"? When corrected, they usually give a few other weak answers ranging from jobs to school assignments. The girls just roll their eyes as the guys once again prove their general cluelessness to life.

Of course, that most important speech is the one that climaxes with the words, "Will you marry me"? Rhetoric class emphasizes finding the most effective means of persuasion. Lunch at McDonald's is usually not the most effective place for proposing to a girl. Rhetoric class emphasizes a combination of *logos*, *pathos*, and *ethos*.

Logos has reference to the rational content of the speech (a real challenge for most guys). The young man needs to have some rational reasons for the girl answering "Yes," but she will not generally be persuaded by a rational argument like this: "You should marry me so that you don't end up being an old maid," or "You should consider yourself lucky since I am proposing to you."

Pathos is the emotional appeal. Passionless language does not move the soul. If the person speaking seems to lack passion, the audience is unmoved. The speech-maker or proposing young man must convey emotion. His body language, hence the popularity of the kneeling on a knee, the look in his eye, the tone of voice, as well as the words he uses all work to persuade the audience of one. (He might break into singing, "I can't live, if living is without you" or some other worthwhile love song, but only if that enhances the emotional appeal.)

Ethos has reference to the character of the speaker. If the girl knows that the guy is a two-timer, an unemployed bum, and an avid avoider of water and soap combinations, she will not likely be persuaded by a rational and emotional appeal. Girls rarely accept marriage proposals from strangers. Even the virtuous pagans emphasized the importance of character. Rhetorical content is not separated from the heart of the speaker.

Rhetoric moves and changes the world. Girls say, "Yes." Buyers say, "I'll take two of them." Voters say, "I'm voting for candidate X." And audiences nod and applaud in affirmation. This chapter on rhetoric is itself, hopefully, moving you to a favorable conclusion. Rhetoric is also a vital tool for advancing the Kingdom of God. Holy Scripture is a rhetorical document; it is meant to persuade. St. Luke, in Acts 1, says that his prequel to Acts (the Gospel of Luke), contains many "decisive proofs [τεκμηρίοις]" of Jesus' resurrection. Additionally, Paul says in chapter 1 of Romans that he is not ashamed of the Gospel because it is the power of God for salvation to everyone who believes.

Let's look a bit closer at both Luke and Paul's claims. Luke, a Gentile, a doctor and man of science, and a first rate historian, bases both his Gospel and his story of the early church in terms of persuasive evidence. (By the way, four out of five doctors agree that death has no cure. The fifth doctor died, so he is evidence that death has no cure.) Yet, Luke writes of tangible proofs of Jesus's teaching, actions, and resurrection.

Paul was at home both in the Jewish synagogue tradition and in the Greek academy. He was also a Roman citizen. He knew the politics and philosophy of his age and the religion of his people. In light of all the forces surrounding him, Paul says that he is not at all hesitant, embarrassed, or in need of making excuses for the Christian answer to all of man's problems and needs. That answer is the gospel.

Luke, Paul, and the other authors of Scripture were rhetors—that is, speakers and writers who were aiming at persuading audiences, which ranged from individuals, to church leaders, to congregations, and on to gatherings of unbelievers. The study of rhetoric, then, has the goal of equipping our students to evangelize the lost, give a defense of the faith to objectors and doubters (apologetics), and give instruction in the faith to fellow believers. God's truth is God's truth whether spoken clearly or garbled. God's truth is God's truth whether the speaker is interesting or boring. God's truth is what is essential, non-negotiable, and unchangeable. Nonetheless, we ought to present the truth in a way that is clear and compelling.

We should remember that nobody can accept Jesus Christ as Lord and Savior, apart from the regenerating work of the Holy Spirit. As Paul said, "I planted, Apollos watered, but God gave the increase" (1 Corinthians 3:6). The Holy Spirit can save a lost person through a poor speaker using a bad translation of an obscure verse in a stuffy, moldy smelling church building. But the glorious double truth is this: God is sovereign, and man is responsible.[4] Christians have the responsibility to learn, use, cultivate, improve upon, and teach the best possible means of persuasion. That means rhetoric class. That means learning from dead ancient Greeks like Aristotle and using modern devices like laptops. Our job in the long term: discover what is in us that can be cultivated into sharper tools for advancing the church and preaching the good news of Jesus Christ.

Assignment for Chapter 8

Read 1 Peter 3:15–16. Notice that the argument for which we ought to prepare concerns our *hope*. Notice also *how* we ought to defend the our hope: "with gentleness and respect," or another translation might read "with humility and fear [πραΰτητος καὶ φόβου]." What kind of

[4] J. I. Packer, *Evangelism and the Sovereignty of God*, rev. ed. (Downers Grove, IL: InterVarsity Press, 2012).

training and preparation do we need in order to defend the hope in us to everyone who asks?

Scripture Memorization

1 Peter 3:15–16:

> In your hearts honor Christ the Lord as holy, always being prepared to make a defense to anyone who asks you for a reason for the hope that is in you; yet do it with gentleness and respect, having a good conscience, so that, when you are slandered, those who revile your good behavior in Christ may be put to shame.

Recommended Reading Assignments

James Nance, "The Why and How of Logic" in Douglas Wilson, ed., *Repairing the Ruins: The Classical and Christian Challenge to Modern Education* (Moscow, ID: Canon Press, 1996).

Douglas Wilson, "The How and Why of Rhetoric" in Douglas Wilson, ed., *Repairing the Ruins: The Classical and Christian Challenge to Modern Education* (Moscow, ID: Canon Press, 1996).

CHAPTER NINE

2ND PERIOD: LATIN, REALLY?

Parenting involves lots of pioneering-like adventures or challenges. The world is a wilderness journey and trying to nurture children through a wilderness journey calls us to pray and work (or, in Latin, *ora et labora*). Sometimes as parents, it seems like there are no paths through the wilderness. At other times, the paths are very rough and barely carved. Some paths are so narrow that a person might pass through, but an oxcart cannot.

Two bits of advice about this wilderness journey: know where you are going, and know what tools you need. We should realize there have been many trailblazers who have gone before us. Hebrews 11 applies this idea to the Christian faith. By faith, the Old Testament heroes "subdued kingdoms, worked righteousness, obtained promises, stopped the mouths of lions" and so on (Hebrews 11:33). We look to those spiritual trailblazers and try to apply their faith and actions to our own situations. We recognize that the hungry lions we face are different from those Daniel faced. Likewise, a parent in America today faces a different set of specific problems than what Moses confronted in Egypt. Yet, the faith heroes of Hebrews 11 can point us in the right direction.

Preparing for the future and preparing your children for the future must involve a backward glance. You do not abandon or discard what is of value from the past. In fact, it is by looking to the past that we find fresh vision for the future. The tools of the past are what aided ancient heroes of the faith to where they were going. We look to the past to understand the present and lead us into the future. We draw from old ideas and tools, learning from the past mistakes of others as well as our own. In short, we look to the heroes of antiquity to understand where we are going.

Last chapter we dealt with Logic and Rhetoric: premises and persuasions. In this chapter we will take those two learning tools and attempt to persuade you to believe in the priority of Latin and Greek in your child's education. Let us state our conclusion—our main point of this chapter—right up front: *your children should learn Latin and Greek during their time in school.*

The remainder of this chapter will contain all the premises that support this conclusion. We will follow the *modus ponens* logical form we learned in the last chapter:

1. <u>If</u> P, <u>then</u> Q.
2. P.
3. <u>Therefore</u>, Q.

Here how our argument is structured:

1. <u>If</u> Latin and Greek are necessary for education, <u>then</u> your children should learn Latin and Greek during their education.
2. Latin and Greek are necessary for education.
3. <u>Therefore</u>, your child's education should prioritize Latin and Greek.

Before we explain our premises that support the "P" in our syllogism above, we first need a history lesson (Ben loves history).

Latin was central to education for centuries. However, the very fact that something was done for a long, long time is, in itself, a good reason for seriously considering it. We should not hastily reject tradition, custom, and "the way things have always been" because we are moderns, post-moderns, or whatever is post-post-modern (meta-modern?). Nor should uphold tradition simply because that is the way grandpa and grandma did it. In Logic class, we learn that this is a fallacy called *the appeal to tradition* fallacy.[1]

---

[1] This fallacy rests its entire conclusion on the antiquity of any given tradition. However, simply because a tradition has been upheld for decades, centuries, or even millennia isn't a valid reason to affirm such tradition. We'll leave to your imagine certain "traditions" for which the *appeal to tradition* fallacy would be especially heinous to employ.

For nearly two-thousand years, Latin was the common tongue of the Greco-Roman and Western European worlds—that is, it was the "common tongue" spoken ubiquitously as far southwest as Morocco and as far northeast as modern-day Ukraine, roughly from the first century BC to the 18th century AD—nineteen-hundred years! Recently as the early twentieth century, C. S. Lewis carried on a letter exchange with an Italian priest in Latin, since neither knew the other's native language well.[2] Authors well into the 20th century assumed that readers knew or could translate Latin words, phrases, and interact with primary Latin documents.

Pragmatic (Lesser) Reasons for Learning Latin

When we begin inquiring into the worth or need for Latin, we must recognize that we will have to borrow Latin to question Latin. Somewhere around sixty to eighty percent of our English words are derived from Latin. Case in point: the word percent is from the Latin words per, meaning "through," and cent, meaning "100."

In other words, a person cannot effectively make a case against Latin without heavily relying on Latin. Latin, therefore, instructs in deciphering words'—English words— roots and meanings.

In many scientific and academic fields, Latin words and phrases are ever present. The scientific names of plants and animals, many theological and literary phrases, legal terms, and historic slogans and mottos are mostly in Latin. Latin words and phrases are omnipresent (another Latin word) in our culture.

A large amount of the words of the classical and concert music that is still performed in music halls is in Latin. Latin words are found on our money, our national buildings, and monuments. Even our Marines Corps is defined by the Latin motto *Semper Fidelis*—always faithful.

All of these reasons would, I hope, convince many of you. Here is another: Latin is relatively difficult to learn and master. It's only difficult because it's different. In all reality, Latin is easier to learn than

---

[2] See *The Latin Letters of C. S. Lewis* (South Bend, IN: St. Augustine's Press, 2016).

English; once you learn the rules, the rules, more or less, remain constant (not so with English!).

However, Latin, like mathematics, it involves extreme care and discipline in order to get the right form of the word in the right place. Close, sorta, almost, kinda, and "like" just don't pass muster in Latin class. A good effort on the part of a student, with an almost correct ending of a nearly correct word gets a big red "X" on the page. Latin is not taught to boost personal self-worth and self-esteem. It is a discipline that calls for the same amount of rigor and dedication as training for cross country running or mastering the violin.

If a student skims across the assignments in a well taught Latin class without having to study, he is probably named Julius, lives in Italy, wears a toga, dreams of military conquests, and has an interest in politics. Latin trains the student to think systematically and to be painstakingly precise. The Latin student must demonstrate with utmost scrupulousness the exact declensions of nouns and conjugation of verbs.

Training in Latin is then preparing students for the study of law, medicine, math, business, and technological fields, as well as the liberal arts.

Less-Pragmatic (Better) Reasons for Learning Latin

There are several non-pragmatic reasons for studying Latin not mentioned in this chapter. It would assist to mention them.[3]

First, learning Latin strengthens language acquisition, which is the skill of *learning anything*. In other words, knowing Latin establishes the mental habits you need to learn and decipher new tasks.

Second, Latin will strengthen your English *rhetoric* skills. Latin grammar and syntax makes you hyper aware of the grammar and syntax of your native language. You'll find yourself subconsciously correcting your family members:

---

[3] This section makes heavy use of a wonderful YouTube video produced by Classical Conversations. It's called "3 Reasons to Study Latin (for Normal People, Not Language Geeks)."

"Uncle Charles, you said 'I.' It's 'me.'"
Confused, Uncle Charles responds, "Huh?"
"You said, 'I bought some treats for you and I.' You should have used the *accusative* "me"—"you and *me*."

As a result of this hyperawareness, your English rhetoric will become more fit, trim, and clear.

Lastly, learning Latin will grant you wisdom. When you learn Latin you make inferences based upon patterns that are easily identifiable. This plays into the first reason, but we can apply it to a pattern of observing. Latin trains the mind to conceptualize a single term within the context of a multiplicity of other terms, seeing its relationship with them all. This habit of thinking extends itself beyond Latin into many aspects of life—especially into the relationships we share with loved ones.

Only Latin?

Classical Christian schools usually teach Latin. By the way, some teach what is called Ecclesiastical Latin (Latin as developed and taught by the Christian Church through history), while others teach Classical Latin. Prim, proper, scholarly Latin teachers get into violent arguments, shouting Latin insults back and forth, and occasionally rolling in the floor punching each other out over this issue.

Some classical schools teach Greek, too. A strong case can be made for teaching Greek, whether it is Koine Greek or Classical Greek. Again, Greek scholars wage intramural wars over this. Classical Greek would enable you to read Homer's *Iliad* or Plato's *Republic* in the original (the secret heart desire of all literature teachers), while Koine Greek would enable you to read the New Testament in the original (a blessing to all Bible students). Neither form of older Greek enables you to bargain with the street vendor in Athens trying to sell you a cheap replica of Achilles' shield.

The main argument against teaching Greek instead of Latin is that Greek involves a different alphabet, and it's very difficult. (The word alphabet comes from two Greek words that the Romans later Latinized.) The main advantage of learning Greek after a thorough grounding in

Latin is that the student has had the discipline of learning an inflected language through Latin.

Being able to read, better interpret, and then better teach the New Testament is a powerful argument for Greek class. Years ago, Ben walked into a classroom full of seniors and they were stumbling through trying to read 1 John out loud. Of course, we know that there are high school kids all around us who cannot read well, cannot read out loud, and who do not even know what John's first epistle is. These students were stumbling, struggling, and mispronouncing words, but they were reading the Word of God in the original. The argument for and blessings of learning even a bit of Hebrew would be the same.

Two comments on modern foreign language studies. First, any thorough foreign language study is beneficial to a student. Any foreign language study will increase the student's discipline in learning, command of vocabulary, memory skills, and ability to take on additional language studies. So, studies in Danish, Afrikaans, Tagalog, Arabic, Elvish, or even English as spoken in the American South,[4] are all useful.

To make a comparison, let us consider the piano (which considering is better than moving). The piano is probably the best instrument to learn for mastering music. From there, a student can branch out to other instruments, such as French horns, clarinets, or cellos. If the student opts to drop music studies, he can take up playing drums. But a student can begin music training with an instrument other than the piano. You can start with the trumpet, guitar, or violin (as long as there are no neighbors that are close), but the piano is still the most versatile instrument to begin with.

In similar manner, Latin (and Greek) is advantageous as the beginning foreign language. Latin is called a Romance language. That does not imply that Latin studies lead to inappropriate hugging, kissing, and holding hands in class, although it has happened before. The word "Romance" derives from "Roman"—romance.

---

[4] Really useful for reading Mark Twain, Flannery O'Connor, and William Faulkner. See Cleanth Brooks, *The Language of the American South* (University of Georgia Press, 2007).

Basically, many of the places conquered, controlled, and taxed by Romans, whose common tongue was Latin, eventually gave birth to linguistic children. And so, Latin is a great foundation for learning Italian, Spanish, French, Portuguese, Romanian, and quite a few other obscure languages. English is derived from Germanic languages, but both English and German borrowed heavily from Latin (and Greek), in part since Roman armies had their sandaled feet securely placed on Albion and Teutonic necks. For more on that story, see Julius Caesar's *Gallic Wars* or Tacitus' *Germania.* Any foreign language is good, but Latin still wins the toss.

The final issue is when to begin Latin (or any foreign language study). We recommend students to begin Latin studies young, really young. That means the lower elementary classes. It is great when children in kindergarten and first and second grades learn their numbers in Latin and a few songs and jingles. By third grade, the need to start actually learning the language.

Remember: elementary school is grammar school. The prime learning skill and trait of a child that age is memorization. Latin words, chants, and endings are all teachable and learnable. Older students, even up through high school and college, benefit from beginning Latin courses. A smattering is better than nothing. Even one year of Latin study will yield countless rewards.

Assignment for Chapter 9

Read John 19:17–20. Recognize how the New Testament grew out of the Hebrew, Greek, and Latin cultures. Pray for your children's language skills. Pray for your own language skills.

Scripture Memorization

1 Cor 12:8–11:

> For to one is given through the Spirit the utterance of wisdom, and to another the utterance of knowledge according to the same Spirit, to another faith by the same Spirit, to another gifts of healing by the one Spirit, to

> another the working of miracles, to another prophecy, to another the ability to distinguish between spirits, to another various kinds of tongues, to another the interpretation of tongues. All these are empowered by one and the same Spirit, who apportions to each one individually as he wills.

Recommended Reading Assignments

E. Christian Kopff, *The Devil Knows Latin: Why America Needs the Classical Tradition* (Wilmington, DE: Isi Books, 1999).

Tracy Lee Simmons, *Climbing Parnassus: A New Apologia for Greek and Latin* (Wilmington, DE: Isi Books, 2002).

CHAPTER TEN

3RD PERIOD: HISTORY CLASS

Listen to William Faulkner for a moment and think about what he says,

> For every Southern boy fourteen years old, not once, but whenever he wants it, there is the instant when it's still not yet two o'clock on that July afternoon in 1863, the brigades are in position behind the rail fence, the guns are laid and ready in the woods and the furled flags are already loosened to break out and Pickett himself with his long oiled ringlets and his hat in one hand probably and his sword in the other looking up the hill waiting for Longstreet to give the word and it's all in the balance, it hasn't happened yet, it hasn't even begun yet, it not only hasn't begun yet but there is still time for it not to begin against that position and those circumstances.[1]

The Rest Is History

It is not just that history is often forgotten or ignored, but *historical consciousness* is forgotten. We pray that African American students consciously remember the deplorable slavery that supported the birth of our nation, the 1965 march at Selma, and the assassination of Dr. King; that Native American students feel pain over the loss of their lands and the massacre at Wounded Knee; that students of British origin are still stirred at the mention of King Alfred the Great and the Battle at White Horse; and that all American students still ache over Valley Forge, Pearl Harbor, and the World Trade Center.

---

[1] William Faulkner, *Intruder in the Dust* (New York: Random House, 1948), 194.

But do we have a historical consciousness? What is a historical consciousness anyways? Or is history class just another class that some like and some have to endure?

If a modern-day Rip Van Winkle were to awaken after being asleep for the last twenty or so years, he would be in for lots of surprises. Along with the technological changes and cultural changes, he would learn that there is something called "The History Channel" on television, and that it is popular. With all its potential, the History Channel is like all television ultimately—entertainment. And if history is not your bag, grab the remote and surf for a better program.

If we compared school to a river, we might compare history class to a place where the river divides—or a watershed, as it is known. One channel of the river would represent students who love history. Whether it is the pageantry of royalty, the monuments of antiquity, or the travails of men in war, history class is a favorite. For others, history class is akin to getting cavities filled.

There are certain God-given inclinations we as individuals have. One kid is fascinated by the sprawled out carcass and formaldehyde-smelling pieces-parts of a fetal pig on the biology table. Another kid endures and vows not to eat sausage again. One loves the poetry of math, while another waxes over the poetry of language. A four-part choral piece entrances one, while another prefers playing full court man-to-man defense on the basketball court.

Good students learn to be proficient in even the subjects for which they could care less, and extremely smart students often excel across the board. But people have different likes and dislikes. The word "History" translates into magic for one, but sounds like "Misery" to another.

Thus, here is the good and bad news for all of us: God loves history. He also loves the amazing world of science, the rhythmic cadences of song and lyrics, the certainty of mathematical truths, and even the arcane world of philosophy and the so-called dismal science of economics. Part of education is learning to love what God loves. That is, we are to love God by loving what He created. That includes the haze giving rise to the name Smoky Mountains that hangs over the ridges and valleys found in the Carolinas, but also to the folk music engendered by the lives of those Scotch-Irish in the Smoky Mountains.

It is okay to like one subject, or one landscape, better than another. It is not okay to loathe an area of creation that God created and has given to us. We educators must also repent for how many times we have taken things delightful, beautiful, and brimming with life and taught them in such a way as to flatten out the contours, extract the flavor, dull the beauty, and wrench the harmony from students. The students, chained to their desks, under threat of failing grades, and mentally and spiritually confined to endure us teachers, then grow to hate certain subjects.

A teacher can take the wit, subtlety, poetry, and fun of a Shakespeare play and create a room full of Shakespearean haters. A teacher can take the wonders of science, the poetry of mathematics, the mathematics of poetry, the sound of music, and the art of art and force feed students such vile recipes of those things as to produce intellectual anorexics. And, horror of horrors, a teacher can open the door to the past, unfold the pageant of history, line out the chronology of our ancestors, and do those things in such a way as to cause students to say really wicked things. We refer to such vile language as this: "History is boring." "I hate history." And, "What do we need to know that for"?

Any history teacher who so desecrates the teaching of history should be taken from the classroom and placed in stocks for all the town to see. Imagine how that would liven up the class. (Kids love to imagine being liberated from classroom drudgery and seeing their soul-quenching teachers sent into exile into Siberia, or stricken with the boils.) Of course, apprehending bad teachers and removing them from the classrooms opens the door to some really great lessons. And those great lessons are found in … history.

Some of those lessons concern teachers being punished, but it was usually the best of teachers. For example, Socrates was put to death, not for boring his hardy band of philosophical neophytes, but for upsetting the authorities. Nathan Hale also was a teacher who was put to death, but not before uttering those words, "I only regret that I have but one life to give for my country." Many Christian martyrs were sent before the lions, or burned at the stake, because of what they were teaching. Many missionaries have died on lands far from home at the hands of people not yet ready to receive the gospel. Then, of course, Jesus Christ, the master teacher, caused endless controversies by his teachings, which led to his arrest and crucifixion.

We are not really promoting cruel and unusual punishments for boring history teachers. Rather, we are suggesting two things: first, everything that is happening in this world—meaning, today's headline news—is a repeat of patterns, events, and situations that have been recurring for millennia. Secondly, history is really a fascinating subject.

God has no need of history. He doesn't think back to his younger days. God lives in eternity. God created History. Genesis 1 shows that at the end of each cycle when God was creating the heavens and the earth (time and history), God said, "It is good." Think about it: God analyzed the history of each of those creative days and pronounced them good.

God set mankind in history. God ruled over all historical events. At chosen points, God intervened in the God-controlled processes of history to re-channel the stream. Angels might have been wondering, "What is God going to do about the idol-crazy city of Ur"? Then God stepped in and shifted the course of history away from Ur and toward His own purposes. Meaning, God called Abraham into a covenantal relationship with a land, a mission, and world-wide salvation ultimately in mind.

God shifted power at one point to Egypt, and then through Moses, shifted it away from Egypt. We see these power shifts going on all throughout the Old Testament. Babylonians, Assyrians, Chaldeans, Hittites, Medo-Persians, and other nation-states rise and fall, wax and wane, ascend and descend—all in accordance with God's plan.

God then raises up a man whose power and personality conquer and unite the known world. He brings men together as brothers and unites them in a common language and culture. We first learn of his coming in the prophetic books of the Old Testament. He was, of course, Alexander the Great.

Alexander the Great made Greek the common language of the lands to the east of the Mediterranean Sea. Alexander, who convinced himself and some others that he was the offspring of a deity, thought he was conquering territory and toppling empires for his own personal fulfillment. He died young, and his own empire split into a group of warring factions. But the Greek language remained, and, as it turned out, Alexander's conquests had been purposed by God to provide the language for the New Testament.

God loves the chess-board drama of history. Knights topple rooks, queens best bishops, but then some bishops sweep across the diagonal events of history to upset the upset the whole board. God loves it best when some strong player, overweening with pride and contemptuous of God, says, "Check" with God's anointed within reach. It is then that God counters with "Checkmate," using the true King to topple the usurper. God also delights in raising up pawns to reconfigure the course of history.

God controls history. God intervenes in history. God has a purpose for history. Some parts of the story are clear-cut. Scripture clearly points out that Pontus Pilate, a Roman political appointee; Herod, a scheming non-Jewish ruler over the Jews; the Gentiles, who were mainly Romans and Hellenistic Greeks; and the people of Israel all were brought into an evil alliance to bring Jesus to the cross (Acts 4:27). Always, evil men seek to bring about evil schemes. Always, the actions of evil men are used and overturned by God who accomplishes His will.

Beyond the scope of Scriptural history, we cannot always truly interpret what has happened in the past. Augustine patiently explained how the impending fall of Rome (as part of the City of Man) was small change compared to the silver and gold of the City of God. Luther and Calvin clearly restored some biblical sanity to Christendom in the West. It was a blessing from God when British and American armies liberated concentration camps, and the fall of the Berlin Wall was an occasion for Christians to rejoice.

But what about the Crimean War? What if the Light Brigade's charge had been rained out, instead of having occurred and then having been inscribed into the history and literature of the British Empire? Had Russia managed, after twenty dozen wars, to have captured and controlled the Bosporus, would the world have been better or worse? What would have been so bad about General Horatio Gates commanding the American armies in the War for Independence? Or would Lord Halifax have been a better guardian of the British Isles in

1940 if the King of England had given him the nod over the quirky Winston Churchill?

Scripture doesn't contain the answers to history problems in an appendix in the back of the book. We are left to sort them out, to think, debate, and question not only what happened, but why it happened, and how it happened. In other words, history class is a lot like math, except for one thing: in math, there always is an answer to the problem. There might be three ways to get the answer, and it might take a whole marker board to work out the problem, but there is an answer. On the contrary, history is a labyrinth, a maze, a puzzle. "Here's the answer," one historian exclaims. "That's not even the question," another rebuts.

I believe that a person needs to read ten books on a historical subject, like World War II or the Tudor monarchs, before he or she can intelligently nod while listening to a conversation. It may very well take one hundred books before a person can enter the conversation. Yet, history class is like an inviting pool on a hot day. Just jump in. Yes, Michael Phelps can swim better, but there's nothing stopping you from dog paddling.

Classical Christian History

The question then is this: what difference does a classical Christian school bring to the history class?

First, an interpretive revision. A Christian who self-consciously applies the faith to the subject will be emphasizing some different events, some less featured people, and some quite different explanations. Luther's theological struggles were more significant than Henry VIII's marriage cycles. Presbyterian preacher and theologian John Witherspoon's theological explanation of the cause for independence is more correct than the unbelieving Thomas Paine's views. George Whitefield was, in some ways, a founding father of America, just as George Washington was. The theological justification of chattel slavery and prejudice was deplorable and hypocritical of Christians throughout America. J. Gresham Machen's battle for Christian belief in the 1920s and 1930s has more long-term significance that FDR's New Deal. The death of C. S. Lewis on November 22, 1963 might be more memorable in time than the assassination of President John Kennedy that same day.

Sometimes, Christians are really happy with getting "our view" of history in the classroom rather than the views commonly taught in public school, or in the broader culture. Sometimes Christians think that Christian schools are teaching "the truth" in history, rather than agenda-driven propaganda. Sometimes Christians divide historians into Saints and Secular Humanists.

We should appreciate what Christian teachers and Christian history textbooks do to restore some balance and sanity to history. We ought to favor "our facts" over "their facts." But if our interpretive revision is a prescribed, then we are not doing history—we are indoctrinating with our set of simplistic doctrines.

It looks like this: "Students, you are here to think about history. Here are the ten things that I want you to accept, believe, and not question. Now, aren't you glad that you are not in a public school being brainwashed by the atheists, humanists, and statists"?

This leads to step two: in a classical Christian school, history returns to Herodotus' vision of inquiry. Herodotus of Halicarnassus is called the *pater historiae* ("the Father of History"). He wrote a massive account of the Greeks and surrounding cultures. The point of the book was the Greco-Persians wars. His book is called *The Histories*. (His publisher wasn't concerned about the market appeal of a catchy title.)

The Greek word that Herodotus used for his book's intent was *historia*, which means inquiry. From *historia* we get the word "history," but we often reduce the word history to a list of dates and names of dead people. However, when you read Herodotus' *The Histories*, it reads much like a Homeric epic—lively, painstakingly descriptive, and jammed with information. Herodotus' historical method compels us not to forget inquiry, questioning, researching, and delving into the why's and how's of the past.

Christians should be precise. We should debate which angle of the Reformation was more correct and more successful. Lutherans, Calvinists, Anglicans, and Anabaptists all had different visions of where the Reformation should begin and end, and so do their spiritual heirs.[2] Christians, even American Christians, can ponder the rightness of rebellion against ruling authorities, such as when our Founding Fathers banded together against King George III. Christians can weigh the pros and cons of empires—Roman, British, or American. Christians can differ on the successes or failures of various forms of and applications of government, even at the risk of embracing monarchy. What classical Christian schools cannot do is stifle on-going inquiry, debate, and even the changing of views.

The third difference or emphasis in a classical Christian school is the use of sources. The often-used term for this is *ad fontes*. (There's that Latin slipping in again.) *Ad fontes* means "to the sources"—literally, "to the fountain." Part of the vast reading of literature in a classical Christian school will entail reading primary sources and older defining historical accounts.

Simply put, a primary source is a written account of a battle or the life of a person written by someone who was in the trenches, in the political arena, or at least sitting on the front row of the historical drama. Primary sources also include the documents, letters, notes, and newspaper accounts of events. A secondary source in history is the retelling of the story from long ago written by a person sitting in front of a computer (or typewriter for an older book) in an air-conditioned office. Both primary and secondary sources can be well written or poorly written, heavily skewed and biased or impartial, or highly factual or inaccurate.

Students need both. Students even possibly need history textbooks. Textbooks tend to kill and skin the historical event and then stretch out and tan the hide of history so that it only barely resembles the original animal. But for maps, chronologies, pictures, names, dates, definitions and some connecting texts, the history book is useful.

Better than a history text on the ancient Greeks is two thick volumes—one written by Herodotus and the other by Thucydides. Better than a textbook's coverage of the Constitutional Convention and the ratifying process is a collection of documents, including the Articles

---

[2] Not to mention the "hows" and "whys" of the 1024–1200 east-west schism!

of Confederation, the Constitution and Bill of Rights, and a couple of dozen of the essays from *The Federalist Papers*.[3]

History needs on-going thought, analysis, and interpretation. But the foundation for those things is found in going back to where the stream begins. *Ad fontes*!

Assignment for Chapter 10 History

Read Acts 1:1–3. Luke is *the* New Testament historian. He is a model for how historical research should be done. The whole book of Acts is a history of the early church. What is the role of history in our church lives and in the education of your children?

Scripture Memorization

Hebrews 12:1–2:

> Therefore, since we are surrounded by so great a cloud of witnesses, let us also lay aside every weight, and sin which clings so closely, and let us run with endurance the race that is set before us, looking to Jesus, the founder and perfecter of our faith, who for the joy that was set before him endured the cross, despising the shame, and is seated at the right hand of the throne of God.

Recommended Reading Assignments

Stephen Mansfield, *More Than Dates and Dead People* (Nashville: Cumberland House, 2000).

Ben House, *Punic Wars and Culture Wars: Christian Essays on History and Education* (Location: Covenant Media Press, 2008).

Christopher Dawson, *The Dynamics of World History* (New York: Sheen and Ward, 1956).

---

[3] See George Grant, ed., *The American Patriot's Handbook* (Naperville, IL: Cumberland House, 2016).

Chapter Eleven

4th Period: For the Good of Humanity

> The humanities cannot be dismissed. Far from being outmoded, they are eternally relevant precisely because they are the arts of communication, the arts of continuity, and the arts of criticism. Language remains the indispensable medium within which we move and breathe. History provides the group memory which makes the communal bond possible. Philosophical criticism is the only activity through which man's self-reflection modifies the conditions of his existence. The cup of the humanities, therefore, must be the vessel from which we drink our life.[1]

A Love Affair with Books

The Humanities teacher primarily should not try to help students prepare for college. The classical Humanities teacher is not primarily teaching writing skills nor improving reading comprehension. The Humanities teacher should not seek to improve ACT or SAT college entrance test grades. The Humanities teacher should not try to make students smarter, better equipped for the real world, or grounded in essential life skills.

The Humanities teacher's main interest is in relationships, specifically romantic relationships. Some of the love interests will be short-term, even when hope longs to see more a long-term love. There will be that sudden passionate, emotion-driven love at first sight, but there will also be the love that begins slowly and grows in height and depth. In some cases, there will be mismatches, anger, disputes, and

[1] Albert William Levi, *The Humanities Today* (Bloomington: Indiana University Press, 1970), 93.

conflicts. Even these sometimes lead to the most substantial relationships. Repenting and making up is a vital ingredient of love.

There is nothing academic, grade-oriented, and intellectual that the Humanities teacher should seek in Humanities class. It is all heart and soul driven and physically unrestrainable. Humanities, therefore, is primarily designed to romance the subject of books. Students should fall passionately in love with books.

We want the girls to fall head over heels with Homer, Augustine, Dante, Luther, Calvin, Melville, Twain, and Dostoevsky. Likewise, we want the boys to gaze at Jane Austen while also becoming forlorn and heartsick over Andromache, Penelope, Dido, Beatrice, Cora Munro, Cosette, and Katarina.

Humanities aims at the heart. The more accurate word is *passion*—passion. It is feeling, not intellect, that is the target. We want the students to be surprised by joy (C. S. Lewis), desiring the Beatific Vision (Dante), questing for whales, grails, and heroic tales (Melville, Mallory, and countless others), and looking into, up from, and beyond the abyss. We want them to "have a lover's quarrel with the world" (Frost), to have that "knowledge of the heart" (Allen Tate), to shore fragments against ruins (T. S. Eliot).

We want them to know that the worst of times can also be the best of times (Dickens), that the old verities remain true (Faulkner), that we all almost deserve to be named Eustace Clarence Scrubb (Lewis again), that we may face eighty-four days of fishing alone in a skiff in the Gulf Stream without catching anything (Hemingway).

We want them to have the kind of experience that Emily Dickinson used to describe poetry:

> If I read a book
> and it makes my whole body
> so cold
> no fire can ever warm me, I know that is poetry.
> If I feel physically as if the top of my head were
> taken off,
> I know that is poetry.
> These

are the
only ways
I know it.
Is there any other way?[2]

This is a radical approach to education. First of all, note that Emily Dickinson says, "If I read a book." That is enough to convince many students and some moderns to shy away from this. Second, this approach assumes that the reading experiences, poetic and otherwise, will result in some mental, emotional, physical, and spiritual convulsions. This is more than learning the names of characters, plot structures, and various types of figurative language in order to ace a State-standardized test.

Mortimer Adler, one of the great men of letters in the 20th century, wrote books about books. His book *How to Read a Book*, later co-authored by Charles Van Doren, is an landmark resource. He was a key designer and proponent of what is called "The Great Books" program. There are several colleges— particularly St. Johns College in Annapolis, Maryland (non-Christian) and Bethlehem College in Minneapolis, Minnesota (Christian)—that have adopted such an approach to education. He described the pursuit of the classics as "The Great Conversation." By that, he meant that civilization has a long history of discussing key issues regarding humanity, truth, beauty, justice, love, law, and meaning.

We, those of us born from the mid-twentieth century through the twenty-first century, are all just arriving at a party where the topic of conversation has been going on for thousands of years. The task of the student, the new arrival, is not to jump in with the answers. Aristotle, Erasmus, and Jonathan Edwards have lots they disagree on, but they would all have the same look of scorn at the kid popping off with his teenage, pop culture answer to questions that have weighed on the minds of men and women for centuries.

---

[2] Miss Dickinson did not write those statements in a poem, but I think it works well this way and reflects her style.

Learning begins with listening. Listening begins with a teacher and a book. Hear what is being said. Read the whole book. Learn the context. Learn why it was written. Learn about who wrote it. Learn who read it. Learn what those who agreed did with the book. Learn about the opposing answers to the book.

A high school student who works through the four years of Humanities will not yet know all the answers. But he or she will begin to know the questions. The high school student will start experiencing a whole body "so cold no fire can ever warm" them and they will feel "physically as if the top of (their) head(s) were taken off."

The Humanities program is not to help the student get into a college. It is to prepare them so that they know why they are going, or not going, to college. Humanities romances the student. It seeks to cause the student to love books and ideas. As a by-product, Humanities fills the student with knowledge, that is, facts and information. As a by-product, Humanities shapes a student's worldview. In our context, that means a Christian worldview. But Humanities is not primarily factual content or theological fencing.

The name Humanities defines the goal. Humans are designed in many ways that are similar to animals. We are classified as mammals, along with camels, dogs, and walruses. More defining than our commonalities with mammals is our being made in the image of God. We are God-bearers. We are nobly created; we are sinfully deformed. We think God's thoughts after him; our hearts are filled with vain and warped ideas. We are lost and unworthy of God's love; we are saved by and the objects of his love. We can, therefore, love. And in this Humanities class, we have a passionate love affair with books.

The Curriculum

There is no one route to entering into the Great Conversation. There are numerous lists of great books, essential books, books that changed the world, the best books, and so on. But which books are essential to the "canon" of Western literature (and by what criteria one creates such a "canon") is itself a part of the debate and conversation. There are some certainties. The Christian Scriptures, Homer, and Shakespeare, among others, should be on any list. Books that are current best sellers will not be on the list.

What follows is a list of book selections that would be suitable for a Humanities class. The lists are not exhaustive.

A Humanities program may keep 9th through 12th graders separated, but we prefer to keep them together in the same class. Quite frankly, 9th graders are not quite ready for the books, the discussion, and the assignments. Often, they are intimidated.

Good.

A senior has paid the dues, has read more, heard more lectures, jumped in on more discussions. The senior can swagger a bit, knowing the whole process starts over the next year when he or she goes off to college. The underclassmen begin learning their place and learning the material. And the upperclassmen carry them through and, ideally, inspire them to press onward.

We recommend this pattern:

1. The Ancient, Classical, and Biblical Worlds
2. The Medieval World of Christendom
3. The American Story
4. The Modern World: Reformation or Revolution

Below is a list of the books that go along with the courses.

I. The Ancient, Classical, and Biblical Worlds

1. Edith Hamilton, *Mythology*
2. James Jordan, *Primeval Saints*
3. Hesiod, *Theogony* and *Works and Days*
4. Homer, *Iliad* and *Odyssey*
5. Aeschylus, *Oresteia: Agamemnon*, *The Libation Bearers*, and *The Eumenides*. Also, *Prometheus Bound*
6. Sophocles, *Electra, Philoctetes, Oedipus the King, Oedipus at Colonus,* and *Antigone*

7. Euripides, *Iphigenia in Tauris*, *Electra*, *The Trojan Women*, *The Bacchae*, *Alcestis*, and *Hippolytus*
8. Plato, *The Republic*
9. Aristotle, *Politics*
10. Herodotus, *The Histories*
11. Ernle Bradford, *Thermopylae* and *Hannibal*
12. Virgil, *Aeneid* and *Georgics*

II. The Medieval World of Christendom

1. *Beowulf*
2. Eusebius, *Church History*
3. Augustine, *The City of God*; *Confessions*; *On Christian Teaching*
4. *The Rule of St. Benedict*
5. Thomas Cahill, *How the Irish Saved Civilization*
6. Bede, *The Ecclesiastical History of the English Church*
7. Boethius, *The Consolation of Philosophy*
8. *The Song of Roland* (Dorothy Sayers, trans.)
9. Mallory, *Le Morte d'Arthur*
10. *Sir Gawain and the Green Knight* (J. R. R. Tolkien, trans.)
11. Geoffrey Chaucer, *The Canterbury Tales*
12. Dante, *The Divine Comedy: Inferno, Purgatorio, Paradiso*
13. Edmund Spenser, *The Fairie Queene*
14. Barbara Tuchman, *A Distant Mirror: The Calamitous 14th Century*
15. Morris Bishop, *The Middle Ages*

III. The American Story

1. Mark Twain, *The Adventures of Tom Sawyer* and *The Adventures of Huckleberry Finn*
2. James Fenimore Cooper, *The Last of the Mohicans*
3. Nathaniel Hawthorne, *The Scarlet Letter* and selected stories

4. Herman Melville, *Moby Dick*, "Bartleby the Scrivener," *Billy Budd*, and *Benito Cereno*
5. Michael Shaara, *The Killer Angels*
6. William Faulkner, *The Unvanquished* and "Barn Burning," and other selected stories
7. F. Scott Fitzgerald, *The Great Gatsby*
8. Ernest Hemingway, *A Farewell to Arms*; *The Old Man and the Sea*; and selected stories.
9. Robert Frost, poems in *The Poetry of Robert Frost*
10. Eudora Welty, *One Writer's Beginnings*
11. Paul Johnson, *A History of the American People*
12. Alexis de Tocqueville, *Democracy in America*
13. Hamilton, Madison, and Jay, *The Federalist Papers*
14. Sam Watkins, *Company* Aytch
15. George Grant (ed.), *American Patriot's Handbook*

IV. The Modern World: Reformation or Revolution

1. Charles Dickens, *A Tale of Two Cities*
2. Martin Luther, *Bondage of the Will*
3. John Calvin, *Institutes of the Christian Religion*
4. George Mastrantonis (trans.), *Augsburg and Constantinople*
5. John Milton, *Paradise Lost* and selected poems
6. Selected plays and sonnets of William Shakespeare
7. Jonathan Edwards, *The Nature of True Virtue*
8. Jane Austen, *Pride and Prejudice*
9. Victor Hugo, *Les Miserables*
10. Karl Marx, *Communist Manifesto*
11. Francis Schaeffer, *How Should We Then Live?*
12. Leo Tolstoy, *Master and Man* and other selections
13. Fyodor Dostoevsky, *The Brothers Karamazov*

During the four years of high school, the student will be reading, discussing, writing about, and thinking about some sixty or more major books and literary works. We usually never get to every book, and some books are studied thoroughly, while others are given less attention. Overall, enough books are read so that the end result is a wide knowledge of books and ideas. The program improves readers. It makes many students love reading more than ever. It prepares and conditions students for college. It causes some students to become book collectors. And generally, the Humanities classes are fun.

Most important of all, love blossoms.

Assignment for Chapter 11 Humanities

Read Philippians 4:8. What things might be true, noble, just pure, lovely, and of good report? How are such things contained in novels, poems, biographies, art, music, dance, and other aspects of life? This passage does not just contain ideas to glean for education. It is a philosophy of education. Think and pray on it.

Scripture Memorization

Philippians 4:8:

> Finally, brothers, whatever is true, whatever is honorable, whatever is just, whatever is pure, whatever is lovely, whatever is commendable, if there is any excellence, if there is anything worthy of praise, think about these things.

Recommended Reading Assignments

John Mark Reynolds. *The Great Books Reader: Excerpts and Essays on the Most Influential Books in Western Civilization* (Bloomington, MN: Bethany House, 2011).

Richard M. Gamble, *The Great Tradition: Classic Readings on What It Means to be an Educated Human Being* (Washington, DC: Regenery, 2007).

CHAPTER TWELVE

5TH PERIOD: THE WONDERS OF SCIENCE

Rudolph Bultmann once wrote, "It is impossible to use electric light and wireless and to avail ourselves of modern medical and surgical discoveries, and at the same time to believe in the New Testament world of spirits and miracles."[1]

Contrary to Bultmann, Christians ought to think it is more impossible to use electric light and cell phones and modern medical breakthroughs and at the same time to believe anything less than the world of spirits and miracles. In fact, most of our experiences of reading about the New Testament world have occurred in places with electric light.

Still, he points out what is seen to be the great conflict: Science versus Religion. Sometimes, it is described as a war between science and religion. In any war, there are generals, armies, and battles. But in the battles, what is often called the "fog of war," there is lots of confusion, noise, and chaos. It becomes difficult to know what one is fighting for and who is one what side.

In the distant past science was considered to be a sub-branch of philosophy. It was called "natural philosophy." The issue would have been this: what does a frog sitting on a lily pad demonstrate about life, ultimate truth, and reality? Frogs probably preferred the questions posed by natural philosophy to those poised by experimental science. Experimental science was more curious about what a frog looks like on the inside. In science, philosophy cannot be totally separated from experimentation. Merely dismembering frogs is not science, philosophically speaking.

The key battle for Christians in science has to do with origins—that is, creation. The battle is often described as Creation versus Evolution.

---

[1] Rudolph Bultmann, "New Testament and Mythology" in Hans Werner Bartsch, ed., *Kerygma & Myth*, Reginald H. Fuller, trans. (London: S.P.C.K., 1953), 5.

Outside of the Christian community (and even outside of large segments of the Christian community itself), this battle is ancient history. Opponents of Creation Science, Intelligent Design, and any sort of science that allows for a non-Darwinian interpretation is dismissed as being non-scientific religious fanaticism.

Students in a military academy might hike over the battlegrounds at Gettysburg, and science students might scan over the arguments presented in the Scopes Trial (sometimes called the Scopes Monkey Trial) in Dayton, Tennessee in 1925. There are lessons to be learned at Gettysburg and at the Scopes Trial, but few people, other than history students, debate the best use of Stuart's Cavalry or the flaws in John Scopes' defense in favor of evolution.

Science class in a Christian school cannot solely focus on the battles of the past and present, lost or won. It must rather focus on the subject at hand: the various fields of science God has created.

The Classical Christian Science Classroom

First, science is an area where the study of Christian apologetics is essential. That means we have to learn how to defend Bible beliefs alongside modern science and modern scientific ethics. Unfortunately, the current battleground pits science against the Bible; and so, we need to think through how the created order harmonizes with biblical truths.

All of the tools of reading, research, logic, rhetoric, and theology come into play. Also, a thorough understanding of the scientific issues, the latest research, and most current debate points need to be known. "Here is how we answer the unbeliever …" could consume most of our time in the classroom. However, overemphasizing apologetics deters from the entire point of the class—science through biology, geology, physics, and so forth.

Our students need to know the "stuff" of a scientific discipline as well as the debate points related to the course. A science class in a Christian school should be a *science class* and *not* a Bible class; yet, it should be supported by and be informed by biblical understanding and application. Christian students should be grounded in how to defend the faith in every area of life, including science. Further, Christian students need to be alert for where the implications, or logical consequences, of scientific beliefs lead.

Second, science in a classical Christian school needs to be rich in the history of science. On the one hand, much of this history will be encouraging since so many men of science in the past were believers. It was the certainties of Christian theism that opened the doors to scientific understanding. The idea that science really grew and developed because of the foundations of Christian belief is a defensible proposition. An atheist might say, "Modern science has given the world many things. What has Christianity given the world"? A good quick jab answer would be, "Modern science."

Third, a classical Christian school needs to read extensively in the classics in the field of science. Original primary documents by Isaac Newton, Blaise Pascal, Albert Einstein, and others need to be read completely or in large part. Even Charles Darwin and his *Origin of Species* needs to be read. All too many academic fields are warped by the philosophy of "Newism." It is the latest study, the newest book, the most recent scholarship, the hottest work off the presses that matters most and is taught. We are not totally against that. We would love to see this book heralded as the latest, newest, and hottest work off the presses. But in any field, *ad fontes* should be the hallmark slogan.

Also, the scientific classics from the 1700s, 1800s, 1900s, and last year will have errors, miscalculations, beliefs that are now rejected, and disproven theories. But as C. S. Lewis contended, we read old books not because they are right, but because they are wrong in areas different from where we are wrong.

To pick up on today's issues, we have to know the Great Conversation. The old scientific classics are essential for grasping the questions. And, it is axiomatic that you cannot know answers until you know the questions.

Fourth, science has to be structured around the Trivium. Grammar school needs to teach the essential facts of science: bones of the body, names of the planets, and other lists. Logic school needs to make the connections: the stages of osmosis, the steps in the scientific method, and the parts of the food chain. Rhetoric school needs to focus on students doing experiments, testing theories, debating and discussing scientific issues.

Yet, we must keep in mind that each segment of the Trivium is mutually inclusive and integrated within itself in every subject. Chemistry students in high school, for example, will need to master the grammar of chemistry by memorizing the elements chart. They will work on the logic of chemistry by learning how the chemicals react and interact. As rhetoric, application, they will further experiment, debate ideas, discuss verbally and in writing other aspects of chemistry.

An Avoidable Civil War

Science and literature are at war. Let us be clear: this war is unnecessary and wholly avoidable. It is a civil war, wastefully dividing what ought not be divided. Nonetheless, science and literature are at war.

Students in college are often tugged at by the science and liberal arts departments. The war has been going on for a long time. Science offers more employment and economic opportunities. Science promises more ways to help humanity. Science and literature being at war implies that biology and poetry, chemistry and drama, and physics and the novel are the battlegrounds of the war. Believing in this war explains why so many doctors aren't reading Herman Melville, Frost, or Dante on the weekends. The war is unnecessary, and it damages the human soul and mind.

One could also compare this war to the French and Indian War. Lots of times, kids miss the question on the history test that asks, "Who won the French and Indian War"? Thinking of the power of France, they say, "The French." "Nope," the teacher says. "Guess again" to which they miss they miss the question a second time by saying, "The Indians." The answer is that the British (along with the American colonies and certain Indian tribes allied with the British) won the war.

Science and literature are at war, but not with each other. Science and literature are more than allies or co-belligerents. Science and literature are the same army. Both are part of God's created order. Both are intellectual and heart-centered battlefields for the heart and soul of mankind. Both are creations of God; both are under the curse of the fall; both are redeemed and redeemable through Christ.

5th Period: The Wonders of Science

Classical Christian education sometimes gets criticized for being weak on science. Some think that this classical Christian approach to education favors literature, but sidesteps scientific endeavor. In other words, if your child is going to major in English, history, philosophy, music, drama, or some field centered in the liberal arts, a classical Christian education would be beneficial. But if your son or daughter is going pre-med, seeking an engineering degree, inclined toward a life in the science lab, interested in modern technology, graphic design, and communicating, then the classical Christian education is not the route.

The simple answer to this concern is "Wrong." But it has to be granted that the names, the book lists, and the flagships of classical Christian education salute Homer, Shakespeare, and C. S. Lewis more than Copernicus, Pasteur, and Werner Von Braun. Some of this is a volume issue. Just as in an orchestra, some instruments dominate the sound, so in classical Christian education some subjects boom out like brass instruments. Also, classical Christian education is a revival movement. Ever since the Russians launched Sputnik in the late 1950s, Americans have been on a tear to shore up science in the schools. Schools were judged by educators and the population—by their science labs. Herman Melville's writings were dense, old, and obsessive regarding whale antics; whereas, Werner Heisenberg's uncertainty principle of physics was cutting edge.

Classical Christian education has focused on bringing back some missing elements. If a person hasn't had fresh blueberries in nearly a year, he can go a bit overboard on eating blueberries and using every recipe calling for blueberries. Apples and bananas will return to the menu in due time. Likewise, classical Christian education has been so focused on restoring the classics, rhetoric, logic, and Latin, that perhaps science has been given short shrift.

In terms of education philosophy and methodology, classical Christian education can, does, and should produce first rate science students. Logic and rhetoric are tool-subjects, just like grammar and reading. They apply to and enhance science classes. Latin provides the intellectual discipline needed to master science, as well as providing the historical language of classifications. Reading and interpreting literature is another discipline that is vital for training a scientific mind.

Adam Gardener: God's First Scientist

To complete the argument, let's look at the first scientist, Adam Gardener. Adam divided his initial hours of scientific research between botany and zoology. He had a garden to tend and animals to name and classify. Tending the garden, which was the task given by his research grant, involved lots more than just sitting around sampling fruits and vegetables. Adam had to learn the uses, characteristics, and best means of cultivating crops. He was also busy jotting down names for the citizens of the animal kingdoms. "That one, I think, should be called a water buffalo. No, wait. I have already used that name. That one is a chimpanzee, and that fruit he is eating … I call them bananas. Wow, he ate a bunch of them."

Very quickly, Adam realized that he needed a lab assistant. For one thing, there was no one to chat with during the coffee breaks. (Since he lived in Paradise, Adam obviously figured out the use of coffee beans.) Being a man overwhelmed with duties and responsibilities, he did the most sensible thing he could do. He took a nap.

Upon awakening, Adam noted several unusual changes. In his side, he saw a patch of skin on his side that was red and tender. Pushing against it a little bit, he could feel a soft hollowness where before there had been something solid. He pondered for a moment about this change in his body.

Then Eve appeared.

"Then the rib which the Lord God had taken from man He made into a woman, and He brought her to the man" (Genesis 2:22). This is where the gap theory appears in the Bible. Adam probably wiped his still sleepy eyes to make sure of what he was seeing, and then he likely gave Eve a good long look up and down.

Whereas Adam had really needed help for his research in botany and zoology, he suddenly didn't think of that anymore. Anatomy class suddenly became a lot more interesting. And his quick visual comparison and contrast led him to make some conclusions regarding experimental science.

But Adam the scientist didn't respond with a scientific treatise on anatomy, and thankfully, he was on the scene too early to delve into the sociology of gender studies. Instead, he responded with *poetry*, and thus he followed His Creator's pattern of creation. God poetically and actually created the universe. The poem of creation, as found in Genesis 1, is a reflection of the poetic impulses of God. So, Adam responds to this latest creation with poetry. Adam said,

> This is now bone of my bones,
> and flesh of my flesh:
> she shall be called Woman,
> because she was taken out of Man.

Adam poked lightly at the place where his rib had been, looked at Eve, and said, "bone of my bones." Unlike the camel that was nearby, the bird that was perched on a branch, and the turtle crawling along at his feet, this creature had the same exterior covering, so he added, "flesh of my flesh." He then gave her the name Woman, which meant "Wife of Man" because she came from that missing rib.

Adam's statement was poetry. It was the first epithalamion, which is a poem celebrating marriage.[2] It was a love song. It was a boy meets girl scenario. None of this implied any need on Adam's part to abandon botany or zoology. Life in paradise would be the marriage of science and literature.

The fall of man was not caused by Adam and Eve's scientific curiosity. The serpent based his premises on epistemology (how we know and how we know we know), rather than on sound science. It is not good science to stare down a gun barrel to figure out what a bullet looks like coming out of the barrel. It was not good science to entertain a question about God's command.

Adam and Eve forgot the most basic lesson from their marriage counseling sessions. That lesson was this: what does God's Word say? It said, "Everything can go in the salad, but this particular fruit." Hence, the Fall. The Fall led to greater struggles in science and tragedy in literature. In redemption, science leads to greater productivity and the

---

[2] The epithalamion became a traditional form of poetry. See Edmund Spenser's contribution to this poetic form aptly titled "Epithalamion."

literature of this world turns into a comedy, which in literature is a happy ending culminating in a wedding.

Assignment for Chapter 12

Genesis 1 and 2. How do these two chapters provide the framework for a Christian view of science? There are lots of battle lines drawn across the scope of these chapters. Also, the fall of man, as presented in Genesis 3, radically changes the way the whole scientific issue works. What role do these chapters play in sciences of all kinds and other subjects as well (such as anthropology, sociology, psychology, and so on)?

Scripture Memorization

John 1:1–3:

> In the beginning was the Word, and the Word was with God, and the Word was God. He was in the beginning with God. All things were made through him, and without him was not anything made that was made.

Recommended Reading Assignments

Vern Poythress, *Redeeming Science: A God-Centered Approach and Philosophy, Science, and the Sovereignty of God* (Wheaton, IL: Crossway, 2006).

Nancy R. Pearcey and Charles B. Thaxton, *The Soul of Science: Christian Faith and Natural Philosophy* (Wheaton, IL: Crossway, 1994).

Philip E. Johnson, *Darwin on Trial* (Downers Grove, IL: InterVarsity Press, 1993).

Chapter Thirteen

6th Period: Aesthetics and Athletics

> Finally, brothers, whatever is true, whatever is honorable, whatever is just, whatever is pure, whatever is lovely, whatever is commendable, if there is any excellence, if there is anything worthy of praise, think about these things. (Phil 4:8)

Paul's words above provide the foundation for a total philosophy of education and life. On the one hand, some commentators seek to apply this passage exclusively to matters relating to salvation, or as we often say, to spiritual matters. Certainly, Christ's work and the Christian life is full of that which is true, noble, pure, lovely, of good report, virtuous, and praiseworthy. Other Bible students see this passage as having a broader application. They see a mandate here. So, the true, noble, pure, lovely, and so on exists in the physical and spiritual realms all around us. We, as believers, are to shop at the cultural mall of the world and pick out those items that reflect truth, goodness, and beauty.

This philosophy of education and cultural interaction was wonderfully explained by Augustine in *On Christian Teaching*. He writes, "A person who is a good and a true Christian should realize that truth belongs to the Lord, wherever it is found" (*Doct. chr.* 29.29).

He goes on to write,

> Any statements by those who are called philosophers … which happen to be true and consistent with our faith should not cause alarm, but be claimed for our own use, as it were from owners who have no right to them. Like the treasures of the ancient Egyptians, who possessed not only idols and heavy burdens…but also vessels and ornaments of gold and

> silver, and clothes, which on leaving Egypt the people of Israel, in order to make better use of them, surreptitiously claimed for themselves. (*Doct. chr.* 2.40)

From this, Augustine counsels Christians to sift through the goods of the pagans, to discard the worthless, but to "plunder the Egyptians" when those things are discovered that "are more appropriate to the service of the truth." Christians have a standard of truth, beauty, and goodness, and wherever we find reflections of our standard, we should take, use, seize such goods, bringing them into Christian service.

Aesthetic Counters Barbarism

Aesthetic refinement is the answer to the ever-present pressures of barbarism. We are always just a generation from descending into total barbarians. Those of you who deal with junior high boys know that the descent is potentially much more imminent.

Education is, by definition, a means of improvement. A slob doing calculus is still a slob. His education is not complete. Drooling during a job interview might have no relevance to a person's academic training for the job, but drooling really dampens a person's employment prospects.

The goal of education is always a senior picture. Those pictures often show the best sides of students, with caps and gowns in hand, and with blemishes being photo-shopped out. The senior or graduation picture is a symbol of what we really want for ourselves and our children. You can wrestle a robe and a doctoral sash around the family dog, attach a diploma to his collar, and hurry and snap a picture. It might be funny to everyone, except for the dog, but it is not reality.

We really want to see our children complete or made whole through education. We want them academically complete (or ready for the next step), socially complete, and even physically complete. As Christians, we want them spiritually complete as well. Complete, as we are using the word here, is not perfect. Complete would mean that the student is prepared for the next steps, such as college, career, and marriage.

Aesthetic studies provide essential training in completeness. In what follows, aesthetic studies will include drama, art, music, and (you might be surprised) athletics—in reverse order.[1]

Aesthetics and Athletics

We would be able to get the attention of more parents and certainly more students if the topic were athletics instead of aesthetics. The quick answer on athletics is that classical Christian education as a philosophy and methodology provides a more wholesome and robust application of athletic activities and physical fitness than typical public school districts. Athletic programs in Christian education must begin with a theological and philosophical perspective before even the calisthenics begin.

Much of the public school philosophy, which is an echo of the American sports philosophy, tends toward athletic idolatry. Sports often consume, distract, overwhelm, and disrupt the purposes of education and life in all kinds of ways, if not kept in proper perspective. It is strange that public schools are overwhelmed with promoting equality, opening to the door to all children, abhorring any kind of discrimination, and being politically correct—until it comes to Friday night football. At the point, where playing fields, goal posts, and scoreboards come into play, public schools become elitist and discriminatory. No public school would field a team of eleven girls against a team of eleven boys when the district playoffs are in view.

"[Such a] demand for equality has two sources: one of them is among the noblest, the other is the basest of human emotions. The noble source is the desire of fair play. But the other source is the hatred of superiority."[2] For some ludicrous reason government schools despise academic superiority but break the tenth commandment when it comes to the State high school football championship.

Many (non-classical) Christian schools often brandish their Nike uniforms and air up the ball before thinking through a Christian philosophy of athletics. "No Pray, No Play" becomes the Christian

[1] Other things could be added, such as dance and architecture.

[2] C. S. Lewis, "Democratic Education," originally published as "Notes on the Way," *Time and Tide* 29 (1944): 369–70.

answer to "No Pass, No Play." Other than the (no-so-clever) catchy mantra, such Christian schools look no different than many godless public schools during the sports seasons.

Being in a fallen world, and a fallen world where young people are frequently blessed with speed, strength, and agility, and a fallen world where competition on the playing field goes beyond metaphor of life to really seeming like life itself, the whole field of athletics is difficult to manage spiritually. So is every other field of life and study; however, there likely was no crowd ever found screaming and cheering when a student aced a history test.

Athletics plays a crucial role in the upbringing on young men and women. During the high school years especially, God has gift these students to function at high speeds accompanied by great strength and agility. There's a real aesthetic beauty in watching a senior basketball star effortlessly weave in and out to secure a lay-up. There's a real art about an MLB pitcher soaring a small ball at 90 mph—*and making it curve*! There's a awe that captivates the human soul when Michael Phelps is in the pool. There's an inspiring-wonder that ravishes the mind whenever Tom Brady soars a football halfway down the field with pinpoint precision.

Athletics isn't about accolades. Athletics is about aesthetics.

Musica Magnorum Solamen Ducle Laborum

That's Latin for "*Music is a solace of great labors.*" New students in school are often a puzzled and maybe troubled when they first hear the rumors of Ben's classes. Often, they hear it from him personally. Ben has a crush on the music teacher! Thankfully, the truth is that he's married to the music teacher. So, he's a bit prejudiced toward music class, but still trying to be "fair and balanced."

Music, as well as art and drama, are misunderstood as classes. Almost no one objects to elementary students learning to sing some songs, banging sticks and ringing bells in a rhythm band, and learning the names and hearing the music of some famous composers. Likewise, most parents beam with joy over their children's artistic creations and small drama productions put on in elementary.

6th Period: Aesthetics and Athletics

By the time a student in is secondary school, and particularly, when they are in high school, we culturally assume that "the arts" (collectively, music, art, and drama) are the special interest of some and a special niche for others. But most would not consider music class ranking anywhere near chemistry in importance. Music becomes an elective, a choice. It is the cosmetic surgery of academia.

We all have to admit, grudgingly for many of us, that some people have lots of musical talent, some have a measure of talent, and some have little or no talent. (No drummer jokes here.) We all know that some people live to sing and play instruments, while others only become adequate at singing or playing an instrument, and then some would rather have root canals than be made to sing or learn to play a flugelhorn.

So, music becomes an elective course, a choice, a personal preference. It is a mere *extra* in the curriculum of the school. Or it may be an out; meaning, if you take music, you can sit in an air-conditioned music room, rather than having to run laps in P.E. class.

A Christian approach to music, and specifically a classical Christian approach to music, is much different. The Bible assumes music to be a part of life. The Bible recognizes musicians and artists, meaning, people especially gifted and graced with talent. Not every person in the Old or New Covenant community gets a harp or a chisel, but everyone sings, everyone hears music, and artistic works, on earth as it is in heaven, are present for everyone to see and appreciate. It doesn't get any better for the non-musical in heaven. Music exists through all eternity. It's likely that the most musically untalented person on earth gets graced with musical talent in heaven.

Music has historically been an expected part of the training and discipline of a student. And music is a discipline. It is mathematical; it is a foreign language; it is scientific; it adheres strongly to certain laws; it opens the door for variation and creativity. Music necessitates concentration, memorization, a focus on details, and emotional control. It makes a student think within the box, so that he or she must know what the song is to mean, suggest, and show. And music forces the student to think outside the box. We sing of things beyond our experience. Music expands the imaginative possibilities. We sing, "When we've been there ten thousand years bright shining as the sun …"

when we have never been anywhere for that long and have been bright shining as bright as the sun.

As mentioned above, there are the talented and interested, the moderately proficient, and the untalented and uninterested. So, as stated above, music often becomes an elective. But degrees of interest and talent apply to every subject area. The student who dislikes reading, struggles with writing an essay, and hates poetry doesn't get to skip taking English and literature classes. Those who find math overwhelmingly hard to understand and totally uninterested don't get to skip Algebra and Geometry.

Music training is a vital part of education. Music in the classical Christian program is a core subject. Here are the principles that should guide the music program.

Music Appreciation (Not the Class Your Typical Community College Offers)

First, music is taught so as to increase awareness and appreciation of the great traditions in the fields of music. Quite simply, any education is incomplete without a significant amount of exposure to classical music.[3]

Knowing the names of the great composers, the greatest of their works, and the circumstances of their lives and compositions are all part of being educationally and culturally well rounded. Composers were not out of the mainstreams of life, scribbling notes on a page, and contemplating the best place for violins to engage in the major movements of a song. Composers were engaged in politics, religion, philosophy, and society when they wrote. Bach's music not only sounds different from that of Beethoven, but also conveys a different worldview. Tchaikovsky's *1812 Overture* was a really big way of bombastically conveying this message: Russia Beat Napoleon! Chopin was a revolutionary. Handel, best known for *The Messiah*, was a dedicated Christian. The German Richard Wagner wrote the song most often

---

[3] Classical music is, technically, the music of a particular period in Europe called the Classical Period, which lasted approximately from 1750 to 1830.

played as a processional in weddings as praise and worship music for Vikings rather than as a means of getting a bride down the aisle. Classical music, therefore, is a series of worldview discussions written for public performances by orchestras and choirs.

Often borrowing from the great composers, hymn writers took the theology of their day and put it into words for congregations to sing. "A Mighty Fortress is Our God," Martin Luther's great battle hymn of the Reformation, is a call to courage and perseverance and trust in God. "We Gather Together," a Dutch hymn that Americans often sing at Thanksgiving, is a Christian celebration of the freedom that the Dutch won from the Spanish. The hymns of Isaac Watts, Charles Wesley, John Newton, and others all compact and poetically package deep theology and the richness of Christian salvation.

The big dividing point, and dividing implies divisive, in all too many churches today is over traditional hymns or contemporary worship music. Nathan Clark George, a singer, songwriter, and former music leader at Parish Presbyterian Church in Franklin, Tennessee, has aptly stated the answer to this controversy. The issue is not whether we use traditional hymns or contemporary Christian music. The issue is whether the music is biblical.

There are centuries of great hymns that children need to learn to sing. There are still great worship songs being written. Our students may very well be writing the theology in music for the churches in the future. They need to be grounded in the great works of hymnody and great choral pieces of music that glorifies God.

This will also call for learning to sing some Psalms. What is more biblical in music than the Bible's own one hundred and fifty part song book? Just as the church in history worked through Scripture songs by chanting and then adding harmonies and instrumentation, so can our children learn these things. Since classical Christian schools teach Latin, many great works can be sung in Latin. The Advent or Christmas song "O Come All Ye Faithful" is a translation of the original "Adeste Fidelis."

With all the richness of classical music and hymns, there is still all the many varieties of popular and folk music to consider. It is astounding that by writing odd shapes, called notes, on sets of five lines, called staffs, that so many different variations of music can be written. Lyrics, which are poems, are then added to the musical notes and the world is changed, amused, saddened, comforted, and cheered along the way.

Most popular music, most of the music that kids listen to, has great merits and benefits. Sometimes, it is really difficult for music teachers to recognize the musical talents of Lynyrd Skynyrd, George Jones, and U2. Sad to report, but there have been music teachers whose life mission was to lure the students away from Glenn Miller, Hank Williams, Elvis Presley, the Beatles, Sting, and other popular musicians through the decades. It never works, by the way. On the other hand, it is often difficult for students to recognize the worth of Bach, Beethoven, and Brahms. A big part of education is not squelching musical preferences, but enlarging them. Since it is education, it takes effort.

Music classes should not teach musical snobbery (as in, "I would never listen to that") and should make students aware of the vast ranges of musical possibilities. Much of what is great about classical music is the many parts contributing to the whole; that is, the symphonic effect, the blending of the many instruments of the orchestra, the melding or contrasting of the differing voice parts of the harmony, is the key to richness of classical music. Much of what is good about a soloist accompanied by an acoustic guitar is the simplicity of the artistic effect. What is good about a fellow with a guitar, another with a banjo, another with a mandolin, another with a fiddle, is how they combine those instruments together.

If two students graduate from school and one believes that Handel's *Messiah* is garbage and the other would never endure listening to B. B. King sing "The Thrill Is Gone," both have failed. Music appreciation is lifelong learning. It is the application of Sayers' principle of learning how to learn; in this case, learning how to learn by listening.

Knowing the names of the instruments in an orchestra or a jazz ensemble or a bluegrass band is handy. Knowing the notes on the musical scale, flats and sharps, key signatures, and to know how to count music is a lifelong blessing. It is an asset to know that four-part harmony consists of the soprano, alto, tenor, and bass lines, and it is even better if a person knows which of those parts he or she can best sing.

Music Should Be Hands On

Second, music classes should be applied. Imagine a cooking class that consisted of only reading and testing over recipes. Music is meant to be sung and played, as well as being meant to be heard. Preparing for a performance is incredibly good training for a student. It begins with the learning skills of becoming familiar with the material. The same skill set will be applied in all academic subjects and jobs. This is the grammar of a musical performance. The teacher says, "The song goes like this …" and then she plays or sings the song. Then comes the logic of the music. The different voice parts are separated and reconnected. The portions of the music are examined and interpreted. Students have to discern if the song is lighthearted, serious, tragic, comic, meditative, bombastic, or a little of all of the above. To paraphrase John Ciardi's phrase concerning poetry, you have to learn "how does the song mean."[4] Discipline and labor then follow.

The grammar and logic of music is all preparation for the performing of the music. Performance is the rhetoric stage of learning. The word perform literally means "through a form." Mastering the form is essential to every endeavor in life. Students have to work on self-control. Some students melt with fear over a performance. Some giggle, some cry. Some just look like they have been frozen in horror. Performance, rhetorical delivery, of music or any other kind of message involves self-control. No one wants to see a policeman who is terrified or a surgeon who is overcome by nervous giggles. Musical performance teaches the child to stand and deliver a finished product.

The person who never sings in public beyond high school benefits from those performance experiences in the high school choir. The student has learned to be a part of the group. There is the shared sense of brotherhood that comes from the group. In working and practicing together and performing, student learn to recognize certain hierarchies,

---

[4] John Ciardi, *How Does a Poem Mean?* (New York: Houghton Mifflin, 1975).

the rules of expectation, and the concern of pleasing others, particularly the audience, instead of themselves.

Surprising Discoveries in the Music Classroom

Third, music training (and all academic and artistic endeavors) helps in the discovery and development of talents. This discovery is often painful, especially for those who never become good singers or musicians. But sometimes, it is the person who is untalented in a particular area who is the most appreciative. Sometimes, the untalented person becomes the means of enhancing the talent of others. (I, Ben, say those things based on the experience of playing the trumpet for six years and never being very good at it. On the other hand, Colton, a trumpeter of 20 years, has performed in Carnegie Hall surrounded by wonderful musicians.)

There are many disk jockeys, talent scouts, recording engineers, concert underwriters, and others whose musical talents are confined to recognizing and using musical talent. There are even more people who appreciate the gifts and talents of musicians because they know firsthand the work involved.

At the same time, some students will realize that they like music and can sing or play well. They may major or minor in music in college. They may sing in the church choir or sing in a community chorale. They may lead music in church or teach piano to beginners. Or they may just delight in playing a piano, strumming a guitar, or singing just for themselves or singing around the campfire with friends.

Music Is Theology

Fourth, music must be a branch of theology. Not every song will be "spiritual" or "religious." But good solid hymns teach the traditions of the church and the depth of theology. Music made the Reformation. Luther's "Ein Feste Burg is Unser Gott" ("A Mighty Fortress is Our God") enforces a strong, God-centered, victorious faith. Eschew airy, sentimental, subjective weak-kneed Christian songs. Jesus loves us, but he is not our boyfriend. Our songs should reflect the marvel of the Lamb of God who is also the Lion of Judah. Embrace songs that glorify God and His creation. Embrace songs that reflect the power and majesty of God the Father, God the Son, and God the Holy Spirit.

Ars Gratia Artis?

Commonly translated as "Art for art's sake," we could rewrite the phrase as such: *Ars Gratia Dei* ("Art for God's sake"). All that we've said about music can be cut and pasted into our discussions of art and drama. But we would like to make a few distinctions and additions in this discussion.

First, whereas we all participate in music by singing in worship, we do not participate in art and drama in the same way. Whether your worship experiences involve the use of hymnals or singing from the words on a screen, you are singing. Most of us are engaged in music at other times along the way. We listen to music in the car, on our iPhones, while jogging, in the morning while getting ready, at other time while relaxing, or perhaps we attend concerts, recitals, and other musical venues. Often, we put our children in music lessons, frequently learning to play the piano.

Art surrounds us, but is often less noticed. By saying art, I now refer to visual representations. Such art dominates the world of advertising. We recognize MacDonalds' arches, Nike's swoosh, the Coca-Cola logo, and a host of other representations. Art and architecture as found in banks, restaurants, malls, and other places subtlety work to convince us to buy into the product or establishment. When we are traveling, it is always exciting to eat at a new place, especially something local, something not franchised. But there is a comfort, especially later in the evening when passing through an unknown town when we see a Cracker Barrel. It offers a certain Southern, family friendly atmosphere that is predictable and is reinforced by the art, architecture, and background music. Our dining, shopping, and business dealings are centered around art and design that enhances those experiences.

Even if we never visit an art museum, never spend a half hour gazing at and thinking about an art masterpiece, we are receivers, often subconsciously, of a world of artistic experiences. Even if we never dabble in paint, sketch a scene, or mold a lump of clay, we are also participants in art.

So, a classical Christian education would involve us opening our eyes to see what we already see. A classical Christian education involves shaking us from the lethargy that causes us to assume, accept, and buy that which we are immersed in. Art is a representative ideal, an abstraction, a visual distortion of something around us. Even the advertising art that emphasizes athletic, young, beautiful people having fun works within our psyche to create an ideal, a goal, even if we cannot come close to achieving it.

We do not seek to become cynics and scoffers in regard to the artistic cultural surroundings and their messages. We seek to become aware. Remember Dorothy Sayers' key point: the goal of education is to teach students how to think. Along with thinking about Plato, the American War for Independence, and advanced physics, students need to think about the meaning and message of the art that surrounds us.

Second, art does not only need to be not only noticed, but practiced. Some training in drawing, designing, coloring, and painting is yet another educational benefit. Even the most non-artistic person will probably have a yard, a living room, maybe an office, and many areas that call for arrangement. Symmetry, order, arrangement, and color coordination enhance life and reflect upon God's beauty. Remember, a slob can be a believer. He can dwell in a trash heap that he calls home, but the goal of the Christian life is to seek God's Kingdom and the effects of that should be a certain refinement. When Mary and Martha opened their home for Jesus to come, teach, and eat, we have no reason to not assume they worked to make their home presentable and comfortable.

Third, art appreciation and history are vital parts of education. This education should begin in the elementary and grammar stages and should be part of the environment of school. Great art reproductions should be found in every classroom. Raphael's "School of Athens" provides both richness to the room's environment, an overview of the Greek philosophy and worldview, a reminder of the age-old philosophical conflict between the one and the many, and a glimpse into Renaissance artistic achievement.

Students in a classical Christian education should be at home with hearing classical music in the background and seeing replicas of great art. Of course, it is even more fulfilling when they are able to take trips to Europe and witness the originals. Not every piece of art is in Paris or Rome or New York. Local art museums can be great sources for learning.

Along with readily knowing, recognizing, and appreciating Michelangelo, Leonardo da Vinci, Rembrandt, and others whose artistic work grew out of the classical and Christian heritage of Europe, students should be familiar with Impressionists, American artists, art from various folk cultures, and even modern art. All art reflects the views and standards and time of a culture and culture group. All art reveals some knowledge.

Picasso's work will probably not be the centerpiece of our classrooms, but students need to know about him and his influence in the field of art. Along with that, they need to know how Picasso's paintings with random body parts and ugly representations are all brilliant explorations of a worldview. Our rejection of that worldview is not developed from shunning or avoiding art, but our rejection stems from understanding the basic premises and recognizing the art as the outgrowth of those premises. In other words, art appreciation class or art discussions are molded by the theological underpinnings of Christian education.

Fourth, art bring us into the awkward and embarrassing issue of nudity. When Christian education and Christian people blush and turn away from this topic, it does not go away. The world speaks of and displays nudity. The Bible is not silent on nudity and the human body, nor is it always condemning it. Several principles need to be developed in Christian education. First, just because something is called art does not mean that it fits the criteria of art. This is a broad statement that goes beyond exposed body parts. We could call the last three sentences before this one "poetry," but that does not make it poetry. Let's prove it:

Several principles
need to be
developed in
Christian education.
Just because something is called art
does not mean that it fits
the criteria of art.
This is a broad statement
that goes beyond
exposed...body...parts.

See what we mean? That's not poetry. Likewise, there are "artistic representations" that we reject. But that rejection has to be more than individual taste, but has to grow out of learning the forms and principles of the subject.

Furthermore, questions of nudity and nakedness (which we will assume for the moment are synonymous) are questions of appropriateness. We would hate to think that people in medical training would never see naked human bodies. The human body in the mode of the birthday suit is a part of biology, particularly anatomy, and a part of art history. It is also a part of the Bible.

Many aspects of the grammar of anatomy belong to the high school class rather than the second grade. Many great works of art might be in the history textbook or art appreciation book, but would not be appropriate for framing and displaying in the classroom.

When using history books dealing with the Greeks, Renaissance artists, or other times and cultures, it's helpful for students (junior high or high school) to get the giggling over with once and for all, so that we can then get back to the study of history. Flipping through the book, they notice Michelangelo's statue of David. It is an incredible work of artistic genius. Out of a flawed piece of marble, Michelangelo sculpted a seventeen foot tall beautiful statue of David. With powerful hands that could wield a sling shot with force, with deep emotion in his face, this David is standing there completely nude. As much as the art inspires awe, it probably isn't a good idea to place a replica of the statue for in your classroom.

Lastly, many artistic masterpieces, in both sculpting and painting display nudity. A painting of Adam and Eve can be tastefully done, but there is only so much that leaves and Eve's long beautiful hair can conceal. High school is the time and place for serious discussions of art, appropriateness, nudity, and pornography. Watching a documentary on the Renaissance does not give sanction to watching the latest films with nudity. The goal of education is not shielding our kids from the human body, but teaching a biblical approach to sexuality, appropriateness, art, beauty, and godliness.

"All the World's A Stage"

Again, what has been said above about music and about art can be adapted to and applied to drama. Reading, interpreting, and performing plays can be incredibly useful life skills. Shy students can blossom in public. Study, memorization, and performance are all part of the discipline of drama. Working in groups, serving others, and focusing on excellence in delivery of a finished product are all effects of drama. A drama student at Eureka College named Ronald Reagan once used his speaking and acting skills to become President of the United States. Critics who said he was just an actor didn't understand either him or what benefits acting had provided for his training for political office.

A final caveat on aesthetics is in order. Christians have often dealt with the arts by *avoiding*. Music, art, movies, and drama were avoided, shunned, and forbidden. They might, after all, lead to dancing. The Christian retreat, characterized by much 20th century fundamentalism, did not produce a stronger church or stronger commitment or generational faith. It either shackled the gifts of Christian artists or drove them away from the Christian community. It also surrendered the field of art to the unbelievers.

The answer is not embracing every form of aesthetic and artistic creation the unbelieving world offers. The answer is not strategically placing Bible verses within artistic creations. The answer, rather, involves thinking biblically, seeking to apply a biblical worldview to aesthetics. The answer involves teaching children how to learn for themselves.

Assignment for Chapter 13

Read Exodus 31:1–11. Bezalel was equipped by God with artistic gifts that were to be put to use in making the tabernacle. David and Asaph were both musicians and supporters of musicians. The Bible contains music and poetry and discusses artistic works frequently. Pray and think about how music, art, and drama could enhance the good, the true, and the beautiful in all areas of your life.

Scripture Memorization

Exodus 28:2:

> And you shall make holy garments for Aaron your brother,
> *for glory and for beauty.*[5]

Recommended Reading Assignments

Hans Rookmaaker, *Modern Art and the Death of a Culture* (Wheaton, IL: Crossway, 1994).

Francis Schaeffer, *Art and the Bible* (Downers Grove, IL: InterVarsity Press, 2009).

---

[5] Notice that one important purpose of Aaron's priestly garments are to be *glorious and beautiful*. God loves beauty.

Chapter Fourteen

7th Period: Math Problems

If we were to challenge the idea that a Christian worldview in education is necessary, there is one area where, in the past, one might have detected an opening. There is one subject where one might have noticed a hill without any artillery or infantry. We would have made our attack at that point.

Both before and after the Scopes Trial in Dayton, Tennessee in 1925, there have been battles over science. Issues relating to Creation, the origin of man, Darwinian naturalism, survival of the fittest, the fossil records, and so on have been debated, written about, subject to political involvement, and causes of much controversy.

In the field of reading, the use of phonics has been so tied to Christian and home school curriculums that one almost thinks the Phoenicians, not the Hebrews, were the covenant people of God. Issues relating to the character content, or lack thereof, in government schools pushed many people to invest in Christian schools. Sex education, moral relativism, values clarification, political correctness, and others social trends convinced lots of parents to pull out of the government programs. Add to all that, the ever abundant studies, statistics, and surveys that indicate poor reading skills, apathy, ignorance, immoral peer pressures, and physical dangers in the hallways and classrooms of public education.

Add to all that the value of biblical instruction. That is, the importance of studying the Book. In the pursuit of knowledge, we absolutely must open The Book of Knowledge. In learning words, our children must learn about the One who is The Word. If we were to challenge the premises of the need or necessity of Christian education, we would not have felt safe challenging any of the areas above. Science, history, reading instruction, the moral atmosphere, and the inclusion of specifically Christian content and doctrine make a strong case for Christian education.

What about Math Instruction?

Here is where we would once have detected the Achilles' heel: Mathematics. The public school teacher might say that man descended from lower life forms or that the Puritans were religious prudes. The kids in public school will hear things in the hallways, playgrounds, and classrooms that have to be corrected at home or by a Christian counselor. The Bible might be left out of the school's curriculum, but we still have Bibles in our homes, and church provides instruction.

But what about math and math tests in a Christian school? What about the content of math teaching? "2 + 2 = 4," says the Christian teacher in Christian school with a textbook published by a Christian publisher in a class that began with a prayer and Bible reading. Meanwhile, down the street, a secular humanist, card-carrying Communist, atheist, and person who hates phonics is pontificating his agenda in front of his class. And what is he saying?

2 + 2 = 4. So what do we do? What about math? And math is no mere sideshow in the curriculum, college, or career track. Good math scores add up to good scholarships. Math proficiency divides the good students from the great students. Mathematical prowess multiplies the chances of success in many fields. A good grasp of the liberal arts minus the needed math skills spells doom for the many students.

A prayer in math class, even when it is not test day, is good, and math, like our food and drink, needs to be received with thanksgiving. Kids in math class need all the prayers and patience the teacher can muster. But these are not winning debate points.

Should the Christian school math teacher preface every statement with words to this effect: "Let us take these God-given integers and add them to these other God-given integers"? Should the teacher remind the students of God's providence by saying, "If Tom has ten apples and eats two of them, how many will he have, God willing, for the pie his mother will bake"? (Providentially, Tom could eat two apples and then meet a delightful girl who really likes apples. Mom's pie gets forgotten. Or maybe climate conditions lead to quick rotting of the other apples. Or maybe Mom bought one of those frozen apple pies that only has to be tossed in the oven.)

Should we avoid all math problems like these: "add 447 + 219, or multiply 222 x 3"?[1] Or should our word problems read like this: "On Sunday morning, Pastor Jim is driving 20 miles to church at 60 miles per hour. Meanwhile, the choir leader and associate pastor Bob is driving 40 miles to church at 50 miles per hour. How much money should they receive in the collection plate today"? One last alternative might seem to be to forfeit the whole subject of math instruction. Maybe even provide an intellectual compensation: which is more important, we might say, calculus or going to Heaven? Geometry or Jesus?

The problem with such an answer is that the question is ridiculous. Of course, Christian salvation and godly growth trumps math and every other subject. Obviously, Jesus would not have explained algorithms to the thief on the cross. But Christian school is for learning academic subjects. Christian doctrine is re-enforced, buttressed, and thought through, but Christian education does not culminate in the salvation experience.

A Christian View of Math

In every subject, there are vast numbers of details, facts, and processes that are agreed upon by believers and unbelievers. A believer and unbeliever would likely agree that a man named Jesus was executed under the reign of a Roman official named Pontus Pilate. The question is, what does that action mean? What is the underlying foundational principles explaining the event?

One humanist might point out that Jesus shares the same fate as other great teachers, such as Socrates. Another person might see the event as an example of Roman cruelty and the injustice of the death penalty. Yet another might explain that the death of Jesus opened the door to his followers creating a series of myths about his supposed magical (miracle working) powers. A cynic might shrug his shoulders and say, "Everyone has to die." The Christian would agree with the historical fact of Jesus dying under the reign and direction of Pilate, but

[1] 666—See the imminent slide into the abyss if your child works a math problem with that as the answer? Kidding (once again)! Seriously, though, some parents have real fears over that number being the answer to a math problem.

the Christian view, philosophy, or explanation of the event is what changes everything.

Where is math in regard to philosophy? Isn't math just numbers dancing around in equations? First, note that numbers or symbols (the ever present X and the frequent Y) are abstractions. Two is a mental concept. You have never seen 2 (or 359 or any other number). You have seen the word two (or dos, drei, duo) and you have seen symbols such as 2 or II. You have seen 2 apples, 2 rhinos, 2 men named Wigglesworth, and 2 or more things that entered Noah's ark, but you have never seen 2. This is because numbers are mere descriptions. (We can, therefore, rightfully say that math is nothing more than the study of adjectives.)

Second, notice that math has a universal truth value. A person might reject old fashioned morality, but who would reject old fashion numbers? You might travel to another country where the manners and customs are different and the word for two is different, but you could not travel to a country where two is three. A modern movie might offer an alternative ending, but a mathematical problem will always have the same certainty. The guy in the love story may or may not get the girl, but 2 + 2 will, despite plot turns and twists, result in 4.

Cornelius Van Til, a Christian apologist, was fond of saying, "The unbeliever can count, but he cannot account for counting." The fact is that unbelievers at the bank, cash register, or classroom can, by God's common grace, add, subtract, multiply, and divide. They can, while living in denial and rebellion against God their Creator, jiggle, crunch, and work with numbers accurately. They may even be expert mathematicians, accountants, or economists. But, apart from God, they cannot give a basis for why 2 + 2 works with certainty. (Imagine accounting if math were totally unpredictable.)

The student in the math class, whether he is learning numbers in kindergarten or doing calculus in high school, may not pause to think upon the philosophical implications of mathematical certainty. The teacher with a stack of papers to grade may not think of it either. Most of the time, we do not think of the ground we are standing on either. But the ground is there whether or not we think of them; they function the same regardless of how we perceive them.

For practical purposes, we function in a world of philosophical assumptions. A college student can, for a few years, question, ponder, and debate the existence of everything. At some point, mom and dad tell him to get a job. And questioning whether food exists or not is a lot easier to contemplate on a full stomach. For practical purposes, we accept the existence of math. But education involves questioning and affirming those assumptions.

So are there different views of math? Don't all people just intuitively know and accept math? Yes, there are different views and while most people do math intuitively, some thinkers have told us to pull back the flooring of math class and study the foundations.

Let's meet some of those who have raised these questions. Dr. Roy Clouser has written a brilliant essay titled "Is There a Christian View of Everything from Soup to Nuts"? and a brilliant book called *The Myth of Neutrality*. In a few pages of the essay and a chapter in the book, he discusses the necessity of a Christian view of math. What follows draws heavily from Clouser

Witness #1: Gotfried von Liebnitz

First witness called to the stand: Wilhelm Gotfried von Liebnitz, a seventeenth century mathematician. A student asked Leibnitz, "Herr Professor, why is one and one always two, and how do we know this"? Leibnitz answered, "Hans, one and one equals two is an eternal, immutable truth that would be so whether or not there were things to count or people to count them."

Leibnitz believed in a self-existent, independent, eternal, changeless number world. The ancient Greek mathematician Pythagoras and the philosopher Plato both held similar beliefs. This number world exists as another dimension of reality. It is somewhat like science fiction stories where an alternative universe exists side by side with the world we know. We can, however, enter into the number world (just like the Pevensee kids entered into Narnia), and whether we choose to enter or not, the number world structures and governs our world. Even if God doesn't exist, the number world does, and the number world structures and governs God if He does exist. Dr. Clouser calls the number world theory a divinity belief.

Witness #2: Bertrand Russell

Second witness: twentieth century philosopher Bertrand Russell. Russell is perhaps best known for his essay "Why I am Not a Christian." While no Christian or theist, Russell was not an unbeliever, however. Everyone believes in something, and Russell believed in Logic. Logic sets, classes, and logical laws exist. In what could be his creedal affirmation, Russell says, that mathematical logic takes us into a realm which is the "heart and immutable essence of all things."

He also maintained that mathematical logic gives us "the absolute necessity that holds for this world or for all possible worlds." Math, when viewed as this incarnation of Logic, is not "just a class." Math, as an extension of logical thinking, is the foundation for everything. Logic itself, as affirmed by Russell, is eternal, changeless, self-existent, and the thing that governs the world. Logic is God.[2]

Witness #3: John Stuart Mill

Third witness: nineteenth century philosopher John Stuart Mill. Mill was a brilliant, although misguided, thinker. And while he wrote a three volume work on logic, of which the third volume focused on mathematics, he rejects both the number world theory and Russell's views.[3] Mill believed this: what we know and all we know is what we can see, taste, hear, and smell. Mill further notes that we share certain ideas, often referred to as "common sense," about the things around us. Water is always wet, fire is always hot, politicians always lie, and 2+2 is always 4. Everybody knows this, right? (We hold out hope for honest

---

[2] A note: what Bertrand Russell believes about Logic and what is taught in the Christian classroom in logic class are fundamentally different. It is like the difference in a wood carved idol that is itself worshipped and a wooden pulpit from where the Bible is proclaimed.

[3] This is a bit of an anachronism since Bertrand Russell lived from 1872 to 1970, while John Stuart Mill's dates were 1806 to 1873.

politicians, however.) Yes, Mill says, everybody "knows" these things, but they are not independent, self-existing truths; they are perceptions.

It is like these examples: the sun moves across the sky, setting in the west; train tracks that are spaced so far apart from where you are standing merge together way down the track to where you are looking; and trees in the distance are smaller than trees up close. But you object. After all, we can "prove" that the sun doesn't actually set, that the train tracks continue at the same space apart, and that trees in the distance are as tall as or taller than those up close. Those "proofs," too, are perceptions. Even the idea that things can be proved is a perception, and so is the idea that things cannot be proven.

We might have liked having Mill as a math teacher because he denied that 2 + 2 always equals 4. Mill would, if consistent, not have marked wrong any of our answers since he believed that we cannot know with certainty that 2 + 2 = 4. That is a generalization. It is like this: where we wrote this book, in southern western Arkansas, it never snows in April— except that in April of 1980, it did snow![4] Just because 2 + 2 = 4 has been the mathematical foundation for millennia is no proof that it will work tomorrow, philosophically speaking.

You can imagine the utter chaos of John Stuart Mill's math class. Not only would the students be going wild, but parents would be lining up at the principal's office and there would be standing room only at the next board meeting. You can imagine the response of a school administrator: "Mr. Mill, in spite of what you might think about perceptions, for the remainder of this school year, 2 + 2 = 4, or you will perceive yourself in an unemployment line."

Witness #4: John Dewey

Along comes our fourth witness to rescue us from Mill, as well as Russell and Leibnitz. This witness, some would say, "rescued" schools and subjects from a lot of problems. (We dissent. No, we don't just dissent; we, the authors, object strongly.) Our fourth witness is the twentieth century American educator and philosopher John Dewey.

[4] Not just a few flakes either. It covered the ground for an afternoon and evening. Many winters we do not get snow.

Once again, we write 2 + 2 = 4 on the board and ask Dr. Dewey what these marks mean.

"Nothing," Dewey answers.

Maybe he misunderstood, so we write the numbers bigger and point directly at them as ask, "Dr. Dewey, do you see these markings, these symbols, and can you tell us what these marks on the board mean"?

"I see them. You wrote the number symbols 2 + 2 = 4. They might be used to help us understand something, but as far as having a real, eternal, philosophical meaning, there is none," Dewey answers. "May I have the marker?

We hand him the marker and he writes *@#-+=c^. He then asks Colton, "Mr. Moore, would you tell me what I have written and what it means"?

Dewey then points to the marker that in Colton's hand and asks, "Is this marker we are using true or false"?

(I, Colton, admit to feeling a bit bumfuzzled or stumped.)

Dewey then explains, "Asking what numbers stand for or asking whether an object is true or false is meaningless. Numbers don't stand for anything. Asking what they stand for is the wrong question to ask. Every tool, like this marker or a shovel or a number, every theory, like 2 + 2 = 4, and every concept, like 'What does this mean?' and even the language itself, these sounds you and I are emitting, are all tools that we create to help us survive."

I am speechless.

Dewey continues, "This marker is neither true nor false. 2 + 2 = 4 is neither true nor false. That window, that car we see outside, that road, are all neither true nor false. We made them as tools, as helps, in order to function."

Dewey pauses and then continues, "What really matters is this: does the tool work? That marker would not work well to drive nails and a taking a hammer to that marker board would destroy it. Truth is not the issue; rather, it is what works."

Dewey, by the way, believed that the physical and biological world is all that exists. The physical and biological world is, therefore, Dewey's divinity belief, or we might say, Dewey's god.[5]

Witness #5: Dr. Roy Clouser

For the last witness, we call Dr. Clouser himself.

"Dr. Clouser, do you accept as true the basic premises of the previous witnesses, namely, Leibnitz, Russell, Mill, or Dewey"?

Dr. Clouser: "No, I do not. I emphatically reject their positions."

Once again, we point to 2 + 2 = 4 and say, "Dr. Clouser, would you please explain this"?

Dr. Clouser responds,

"We should begin by reminding ourselves that God has created the world we inhabit: the objects around us, the properties they exhibit, and the laws that govern them. We may also notice that the properties things exhibit are of many different kinds. They have physical properties, sensory properties, and logical properties, for example. And there's also a 'how much' to them. That is, they exhibit quantity (the very property we most often confront in math class).[6] We abstract that quantity and set up a symbol system to represent it. And we discover relationships among these quantities."

Ben interrupts, "Are these marks on the board something God created"?

Dr. Clouser continues, "The symbol system, those marks on the board, are our invention, but we find quantities and their relations in God's creation. The reason that objects have quantity and that their quantitative properties are governed by mathematical laws, is that God made the world that way. That recognition is a first step toward a view of mathematics that doesn't either regard quantity as divine or reduce it to another aspect of the world for the reason that the other aspect is divine."

---

[5] And it is Dewey's god that most public schools still worship in their hallways.

[6] The parts in italics are my representation of what I think Dr. Clouser is saying. The parts attributed to him in quotation marks are found verbatim (a Latin word!) in his essay.

"What do you mean by your last statement"?

Dr. Clouser continues, "Leibnitz believed that the world of quantity, the number world, was self-existent, eternal, and true. It was divine; it was God, if you will. Russell, Mill, and Dewey believed other things were divine, or God. And they believed that math concepts, quantity, were a part of that divine order, whether it was perception, logic, or the physical/biological universe."

"Does this conflict just apply to math"?

"This difference in approach, the difference between a belief in the Creator God and other divinity beliefs, applies as well to all theories of philosophy and the sciences: all alike have vacillated between picking explainers from the world that are enthroned as divine or picking explainers that are dependent on others because the others are enthroned as divine."

Colton asks, "And, so what is the philosophical answer to the question of whether there is a Christian view of math or of any other subject"?

Dr. Clouser responds, "The biblical teaching is that belief in God impacts all knowledge and truth. My answer to the question, 'Is there a Christian view of everything from soup to nuts?' is that there certainly ought to be."

A Mathematical Conclusion

There are still questions to be answered regarding math instruction at all levels. Curriculum issues revolve around the use of Saxon math, Singapore math, the Jacobs math program, and others. Questions arise about when and where and what age to teach certain high math courses. Some Christian schools, by the way, have reintroduced Euclidean Geometry into the curriculum and they actually use Euclid's *Elements* as a text. (Euclid, by the way, was a Greek mathematician whose work appeared around 300 A.D. It was a core study for students of all disciplines until well into the twentieth century and its principles form much of the bedrock of ongoing studies in geometry.)

Math is a perennial struggle for many children. Extra tutoring is often necessary, and mathematical ability is often latent, rather than obvious. Good math students in elementary school often stumble and fall when they encounter Algebra. For many, it takes a year or two of instruction and some brain maturity for higher math to make start making sense. It also takes time pouring over homework and usually tears and stress. Math is a discipline. The teacher is always more important than the curriculum or the order in which courses are introduced. That again will involve parents talking with the teachers.

Assignment for Chapter 14

Read Colossians 1:15–17. What are the implications of this passage for math? If all things, including math, were created by and for Jesus Christ and all things "hold together" in him, how can we properly teach and learn math apart from Him?

Scripture Memorization

Colossians 1:15–17:

> He is the image of the invisible God, the firstborn of all creation. For by him all things were created, in heaven and on earth, visible and invisible, whether thrones or dominions or rulers or authorities—all things were created through him and for him. And he is before all things, and in him all things hold together.

Recommended Reading Assignments

Roy Clouser, "Is There a Christian View of Everything from Soup to Nuts?" *Pro Rege* 31 (2003): 1–10.

Roy Clouser, *The Myth of Religious Neutrality: An Essay on the Hidden Role of Religious Belief in Theories*, rev. ed. (Notre Dame: University of Notre Dame Press, 2005).

Vern Poythress, *Redeeming Mathematics: A God-Centered Approach* (Wheaton: Crossway, 2015).

CHAPTER FIFTEEN

8TH PERIOD: BIBLE CLASS

Gavin and Aiden were two twin boys who from their toddler years loved swimming at the local public pool with their mother, Mrs. Anderson. Any time Mrs. Anderson said the "P" word, from the time the twins were two-years-old they would wail for want of chlorinated water and sunburns. They loved just about everything about the local pool: splashing their mother, the outside showers, mom's snacks, and the smell of SPF 50. The boys were thoroughly enchanted. (Later in their life the twins could trace their love for paragliding in the Gulf back to these early days in the toddler pool.)

As the boys grew older and it became time for them to "promote" out of the wading pool to the shallow end proper, Mrs. Anderson forbade them; she feared they wouldn't keep their heads above the water. Swimming lessons were out of the picture. The monthly cost of pool visits already stretched tight the family budget. (Besides, Mrs. Anderson, being prone to excessive worry, secretly didn't want them to take swimming lessons because she herself couldn't swim.)

The 6-year-olds Gavin and Aiden soon grew weary of the local pool—watching their friends with their own floaties in the shallow end. This was perhaps the boys' first taste of bitterness and resentment, bitterness toward their mother and resentment of the pool that once enchanted their joys.

So whenever Mrs. Anderson would say the "P" word, the boys shuddered at the thought of the pool. It was too humiliating for the boys. However, as the years unraveled, the twins were permitted to enter the shallow end—with life jackets. By this time, they were 10-years-old, and all of their friends were somersaulting off the diving boards. Their mother's excessive fear was rubbing off on them. They secretly feared the diving board—hearing their mother's repetitious voice speak of one cousin who drowned while swimming in the deep end.

Some of the kids would call the twins names and mock them for their life jackets. Arguments regularly broke out among the kids, and Gavin even got into a tussle or two (which always left him with a bloody lip). Mrs. Anderson was mortified, and the twins humiliated.

And so eventually they would rather stay home. They stopped going to the pool. Gavin and Aiden never learned to swim.

As the twins progressed into their teens they regularly declined any invitations to pool parties, or if they did attend they would wear normal clothes and sit in chairs (to be sure, at a safe distance from the pool) masquerading as uninterested in the summertime festivities. You can imagine the angst the boys felt when girls invited them to such parties. Those moments never turned out favorably.

Gavin and Aiden went everywhere together, and college was no different. They were both natural athletes, though they rarely joined any teams in high school. They valued a good diet and regular exercise. Their cardio of choice was long-distance running. They both were successful cross-country runners in high school. Gavin had more muscle and thus heavier than Aiden who was shorter and pencil thin.

In the summer of their sophomore year in college, Gavin noticed the university swimming team practicing laps. He admired the grace and the enduring determination of the swimmers, which reminded him of his former cross-country training. Quickly he found Aiden, and they both observed for two hours the swimmers hone various strokes and drills. Mingled with awe, the old fears and memories of humiliation and bitterness rose to the brim of their thoughts.

"Like what you see"? It was a thin, muscular man in his 60s. Shirtless with red trunks. No shoes. Long black hair striped with streaks of silver. He had a thick black mustache (also streaked with silver).

"Uhhh … yes, sir," responded Gavin.

"I didn't realize the university had a swim team," Aiden nervously chimed in.

With only his eyes, older man sized the twins up and down before saying, "You men want to come down and swim with the team? You look mighty fit. We could use a couple more teammates."

"YOU are on the team"?!— Aiden blurted out, not realizing the potential for offending the man— "I mean … I'm sorry … it's just I didn't expect someone your age to be on the swim team."

The man gave a jovial laugh as if he were Father Christmas in the Narnia Chronicles.

"Of course I'm not on the team. I coach the team. Forgive me for not introducing myself: I'm Coach Oikos, born, raised, and educated in America though my folks were born, raised, and educated in Greece. So, again, want to come swim"?

Gavin and Aiden looked at each other with horror. Whether it was because they didn't want to offend Coach Oikos, or some other power was moving them, they found themselves saying, "sure." The twins were both terrified but also strangely enchanted by the water.

The Coach was not fooled. He could tell by their facial expressions they were not confident with swimming. His suspicions were proven true. The twins couldn't even float!

But something surprising happened. The team didn't laugh at Gavin and Aiden. They didn't mock or name call. They genuinely assisted the men. Coach Oikos offered to tutor them in swimming lessons each evening that summer, explaining to them that the water is most certainly dangerous, for all things worthy are dangerous, and the twins excelled.

The next three years of college were a blast for the twins. They quickly rose to top of the team, securing victories for the college at most of the major swim meets. Mrs. Anderson's apprehension slowly gave way to excitement and pride. Twins finally learned how to swim, and succeeded. And Coach Oikos stood watching it all, his laugher booming like Jove.

Bible Class is Not Safe

The Bible is a dangerous book. It is a book whose spiritual waters, in which only serious swimmers can tread, go deep. But even novices can enjoy its shallow end. The Bible is shallow enough for toddlers and deep enough to thrill the adventurous.

Many teachers of the Bible are like Gavin and Aiden's mother: for whatever reason they do not send their students into the deep end. The students, as a result, never learn to swim, averting themselves from wonders of the deep.

Too many Bible classes keep them safely in the wading pool, sometimes out of fear of finding out those pesky "problem passages" like the atrocious raping of Judges 19 or the sovereignty of God in Romans 9–11. At other times, Bible classes have an allergic reaction to anything "academic" or "highbrow." Who needs theology when we have Jesus?

Trivial approaches to Bible class instills apathy within the student for the Scriptures. Why go to the pool if we're not going to be able to swim? We'd rather go home and watch television.

Whether or not they acknowledge it, our students crave the deep end as they mature. They want to think about deep matters. They want to learn how to swim. Keep the teen in the shallow end, and he will ultimately hate the pool. Teach him to swim, and then throw him in the deep end. Then he will explore the adventures of Scripture found only at its depth.

We need new rules for the pool.

Remodeling the Bible Class

> Bible class is not a Sunday School class.
> Bible class is not Bible Trivia.
> Bible class is not a "what Jesus means to me" circle.
> Bible class is not share-your-testimony time.
> Bible class is not a Bible study.
> Bible class is not about evangelism.

Bible classes in Christian schools often miss the mark. They're often quite progressive in their approach, modeled off the personas seen in pop Christian culture, and seek for joy and all the wrong places. They're more prone to assert that Jesus gives us hugs and kisses to make us feel better than Jesus absorbed God's wrath to save us from eternal suffering and grief. The hottest Christian track on K-LUV is ubiquitously heard, and the hymn "Holy, Holy, Holy" is viewed as old-fashioned.

They are often treated as Sunday school classes or Bible studies. Bible trivia is championed, and championship trophies for Scripture memory are coveted. These classes sometimes focus more on "what Jesus means to me" than what Jesus has commanded me. Many Bible classes place the Great Commission at the centerpiece of the class. Such classes are a reflection of many evangelical churches in the Bible Belt U.S.A. Narrow topical, and the oft-repeated, Bible stories are the chicken nuggets and Mac'N Cheese of this spiritual diet. Noah and the Ark. Sampson and Delilah. David and Goliath. Jesus and the loaves of bread and fish. And you can't forget the rapture in Revelation. Just click the "repeat" button, and you're all set.

This approach begets a student who may know all the correct, "churchish" language, but the student lacks legitimate biblical literacy. He doesn't know how his Bible fits together. He's like one who knows a handful of major chords on the piano and can play popular worship songs but cannot read music and transfer his skills to other legitimate, more mature piano pieces. The student needs a kind of biblical knowledge that will perpetuate itself day after day within his own study of the Scriptures.

Only memorizing 50 Bible verses, knowing how many chapters are in the Book of Isaiah, or asserting with epistemological certainty the signs of the end times will not accomplish this.

So what will? Four things:

1. Rules for biblical theology
2. Expositing biblical doctrine
3. Understanding how our spiritual forefathers carried and clarified biblical doctrine
4. Knowing how to wisely apply appropriately-interpreted biblical doctrine to life's most pressing ethical demands.

What we are about to propose is a broad, flexible progression for how a school might structure its Bible class to promote biblical literacy—all structured around the Trivium.

Biblical Theology (Grammar–Logic School | K–8th Grades)

Bible classes in the Grammar School should not present stories from Scripture as unrelated to one another. They ought to view the Bible itself as a single story with a clear, overarching plot and situate the smaller stories within the larger story. This overarching plot ought to be underlined, highlighted, and repeated over and over again. This is the chief "grammar" of the Bible that younger students must grasp. Of course, along with this comes other "grammatical" details, such as the many important characters that play crucial roles in this plot: Adam and Eve, Noah, Abraham (especially him), Moses, David, Isaiah, John the Baptist, and Paul, just to name a few. But once again, teachers of younger students should demonstrate the roles of these characters within the overarching storyline of the Bible, showing them how they properly fit within it. A helpful acronym and chart for understanding this overarching storyline, developed by Dr. Jason S. DeRouchie, is K.I.N.G.D.O.M.[1]

OT Narrative	Kickoff and Rebellion: *Creation, Fall, Flood*
	Instrument of Blessing: *Patriarchs*
	Nation Redeemed and Commissioned: *Exodus, Sinai, Wilderness*
	Government in the Land: *Conquest and Kingdoms*
	Dispersion and Return: *Exile and Initial Restoration*
NT Narrative	Overlap of the Ages: *Christ's Work and the Church Age*
	Mission Accomplished: *Christ's Return and Kingdom Consummation*

[1] Chart taken and adapted from Jason S. DeRouchie, *What the Old Testament Authors Really Cared About* (Grand Rapids: Kregel Academic, 2013).

The main emphasis in the first six years of a child's formal education (K–5) is to have this storyline engrained into their heads and hearts. Young students need to read the Bible as literature, a purposeful story of God making promises and keeping his promises through his promised seed.

In the classroom this doesn't have to look like reading through large units of the Old Testament. Because students at this age have not yet mastered reading, are learning patience, and are steadily increasing their attention span, focusing on the high points of the storyline is appropriate. For instance, by the time the student is in 5th grade, he should have memorized the acronym K.I.N.G.D.O.M and be able to articulate all the major characters within each letter (e.g., Adam and Eve, Noah and Abraham, Moses and Joshua, David and Solomon, Isaiah and Jeremiah, Jesus and John the Baptist, the Twelve Apostles, etc.). The student should be able to articulate how all the characters anticipate the promised seed to save the world: Jesus Christ.

When the student reaches the Logic phase in the 6th grade, he is naturally predisposed to rationalize. It is now appropriate to introduce them to Biblical Theology. Biblical Theology is not simply theology derived from the Bible; it is a specific theological discipline that attempts to demonstrate how the biblical story weaves itself together. Biblical Theology (BT) "studies how the whole Bible progresses, integrates, and climaxes in Christ."[2] BT, in short, traces the most central biblical themes of Scripture's main storyline from Genesis through Revelation, showing the thematic development of these themes as they anticipate and foreshadow Jesus Christ and him crucified.

For example, in BT students can see how throughout the Bible the theme of atonement emerges, develops, and climaxes in Christ. It emerges first when God covers Adam and Eve with garments of skin. This theme is developed through Genesis with the patriarchs, comes to a high point in the institution of the sacrificial system in Exodus–Deuteronomy, perpetuated into the Prophets and Writings, and consummated in the atonement of Jesus Christ on the cross. This kind of

---

[2] Andrew David Naselli, *How to Understand and Apply the New Testament* (Phillipsburg, NJ: P&R, 2017), 231.

thematic study can be repeated with a host of key topics such as justification, sin, forgiveness, feasting, slavery, death, adoption, and more.

In the Grammar School, students understand that Bible is a story about the coming, saving, and reigning Messiah Jesus. In Logic School, students understand why and how the Bible portrays, anticipates, and climaxes in the reigning Messiah Christ. By the end of the Logic Phase the student should be able to articulate how and why the Bible is a story that anticipates and climaxes in the gospel of Jesus Christ, and how it sequentially foreshadows the great salvation He accomplishes for his people.

God has woven these themes into the fabric of Scripture and the world. Bible class is about seeing and savoring these truths. In Bible class it is time for your child to swim in the deep end. But just as the Bible slowly progresses in its presentation of Christ in Genesis 3:15 (commonly called the *protoeuangelion*), so we slowly progress our students from Kindergarten to eighth-grade. In the earlier years, it would be pointless to read through certain passages of Scripture that in later years yield wonderful fruit. Can you imagine slogging through the lengthy genealogies of Chronicles with first graders? Yet, those same Chronicles are jam-packed with biblical-theological anticipation of the Messiah-King Christ that 8th graders can readily see and savor.

This is academic stuff. It is deep. And by the end of Logic school, your child will be an excellent swimmer because of it.

Biblical Doctrine (Rhetoric School | 9th–10th Grades)

By the time your child enters the Rhetoric School, he is ready to promote from the deep end to the deep sea. He will be deep underwater—for a lengthy period of time. It's time for him to strap on his wet suit, flippers, and air tank.

At this point in the Bible class, we propose a two-year phase of biblical Doctrine rooted in the biblical-theological methods of the Logic School.

Now, in this Rhetoric Phase of Bible class students will learn the "grammar" of doctrine. Doctrine class should be split into two years: 9th and 10th grades. In the first year of Doctrine (Doctrine I), students will learn about Revelation, focusing particularly on Holy Scripture. In Doctrine II, students will delve into Christology (the study of Christ), Pneumatology (the study of the Holy Spirit), and Soteriology (the study of salvation).

In Doctrine I, students should begin from the beginning: how we know God and the method of formulating doctrine. God speaks first before we understand and respond to him. We know God by listening to his words; fundamentally, our listening is a secondary step in the this communication process. He calls us, and then we, enabled by his Spirit, respond to his call. Furthermore, we only know God through the cross of Jesus Christ. "No one comes to the father except through me" (John 14:6). The cross colors every aspect of theology we attempt to understand and elucidate. And how do we know this? Primarily through the Scriptures. And our knowledge and assurance of this is based upon faith.

In this phase, students will understand the distinctions between what is commonly called "special" and so-called "natural" revelation: the doctrine of Holy Scripture, the Spirit's inspiration, and how creation itself can declare the knowledge of God. Questions such as these will be answered: how does God speak? How was Scripture's canon formed, and how does God speak through a variety of authors? What about the "extra" books that Roman Catholic and Eastern Orthodox Christians use? A full year is allotted to Holy Scripture because it is the chief source from which Christians draw to understand God and faithful living.

Doctrine II builds upon Doctrine I by introducing the doctrines of the Trinity and Christ: God is Trinity, one God in three persons of equal substance; Christ is both God and man simultaneously. Doctrine II will explain why these two teachings of God are crucial for our salvation. Pneumatology will explain how God's Holy Spirit has operated and is operating within our world, and soteriology will show the student how God has saved and is saving those who call upon his name in faith. Ecclesiology (the doctrine of the church) and the sacraments of baptism and the Eucharist will be taught as well. In all these doctrines, extensive reference to Holy Scripture and the chief figures in the early church who helped formulate these doctrines are made.

Biblical Saints (Rhetoric School | 11th Grade)

By the way, do you know why you believe in the Trinity? What about why you believe in the complete divinity and humanity of Jesus Christ? If you believe in *Sola Scriptura*, do you know why?

The Bible presents us with no formalized doctrine of the Trinity. It doesn't explain how Jesus simultaneously is both God and man. The Bible doesn't tell us that it itself, in the entirety of its canon, is the final measure for life and godliness.

Then why do many Christians believe in these doctrines? If you can articulate why, then you've probably done your church history homework. Doctrine and history go hand in hand and must never be divorced from one another. Clearly articulated doctrines of the Christian church for centuries have been forged in the fires of conflicts between orthodox Christians and heretics.

When the student arrives in the third year of the Rhetoric class, the student will learn about the history of God's people beginning with Christ's inauguration of the church and continuing through the modern era. Since two-thousand years of history will be covered, only broad overviews for the year should be prioritized. In the early centuries of the church, God's people had to painstakingly clarify their beliefs to weed out heretical teachings that damage the soul. By the Middle Ages, ambitious imperialism in the West and the Ottoman Empire in the East threatened the health and stability of the church. Later, in the West the Reformation preserved the orthodox teachings of the gospel while in the East Christianity spread northward into Russia. By the 19th century and beyond, the heretical teachings modern rationalism had seeped its way into nearly every sphere of the church; we are still battling this today.

In this class, students will survey the best volumes in church history while also taking deep draughts of primary documents, and if written in Latin (or Greek) the student should be required to consult the original languages.

Biblical Ethics (Rhetoric School | 12th Grade)

True knowledge doesn't cease to exist within the brain. The very actions of our hearts demonstrate knowledge itself. Biblical ethics is the consummation of biblical knowledge.

The Christian life isn't merely a tack on "application section" that follows one's biblical knowledge. Rather, the Christian life is a crucial piece to one's knowledge, for it is in the Christian life that biblical knowledge is embodied.[3] This is where the immaterial biblical understandings within your head become flesh: our physical faithfulness with God's truth demonstrates the truest sense of biblical knowledge. "Be doers of the word, and not hearers only, deceiving yourselves" (James 1:22).

This is the primary emphasis on the capstone Bible class: Biblical Ethics. In this final segment, your child will be sent off ready to face the world's most tumultuous philosophical worldviews that breed chaotic and destructive behaviors and souls. In Biblical Ethics class the student will analyze contemporary issues of morality from a worldview developed from the K–11th grade years of Bible class.

Your student will think through and discuss how the Bible addresses the most pressing issues of the day, such as abortion, euthanasia, the death penalty, sex and contraception, homosexuality and transgenderism, divorce and remarriage, slavery, self-defense and warfare, and Artificial Intelligence.

As you can see, Bible class ain't for the faint hearted.

Assignment for Chapter 15

We return to Deuteronomy 6:4–9. Again we ask, how can you practically bring this text within your home and shape the way you parent?

---

[3] In fact, Saint Augustine wrote in his *On Christian Teaching*: "So anyone who thinks that he has understood the divine scriptures or any part of them, *but cannot by his understanding build up this double love of God and neighbour, has not yet succeeded in understanding them*" (*Doctr. chr.* 1.35.40).

Scripture Memorization

Deuteronomy 6:4–9:

> Hear, O Israel: The LORD our God, the LORD is one. You shall love the LORD your God with all your heart and with all your soul and with all your might. And these words that I command you today shall be on your heart. You shall teach them diligently to your children, and shall talk of them when you sit in your house, and when you walk by the way, and when you lie down, and when you rise. You shall bind them as a sign on your hand, and they shall be as frontlets between your eyes. You shall write them on the doorposts of your house and on your gates.

Recommended Reading Assignments

John Piper, *A Peculiar Glory: How the Christian Scriptures Reveal Their Complete Truthfulness* (Wheaton, IL: Crossway, 2016).

Kevin J. Vanhoozer, *Biblical Authority after Babel: Retrieving the* Solas *in the Spirit of Mere Protestant Christianity* (Grant Rapids: Brazos Press, 2016).

Lessie Newbigin, *Proper Confidence: Faith, Doubt, and Certainty in Christian Discipleship* (Grand Rapids: Eerdmans, 1995).

John M. Frame, *Systematic Theology: An Introduction to Christian Belief* (Phillipsburg, NJ: P&R, 2013).

CHAPTER SIXTEEN

ELEMENTARY SCHOOL: THE GRAMMAR STAGE

This book has focused, as we said earlier, on the senior portrait. Cap and gown, a diploma in hand, a picture budding with youthful good looks, a pleasant smile, and lots of expectation. The senior student is has already entered the adult world. An adult is there in the picture, but there is expectation for he or she is yet unsullied by the tasks and burdens that accumulate through the years. The senior picture is full of hope. Graduation is an ending that is a beginning.

Everything in the senior portrait hinges on the preparation leading up to the moment the camera lens closes. Eighteen years of home and church and at least thirteen years of schooling have been poured into the form that is now set for life.

The end result is the goal. The end goal is not just high school or college graduation. Marriage, career, and your future grandchildren are all steps. The greater goal is a life lived serving, loving, and obeying God. The chief end of man, the Westminster Shorter Catechism tells us, is to glorify God forever.

But for now, with that little one in hand or in mind, what does elementary school look like in classical Christian education?

Latin, logic, rhetoric, and Humanities are the vital components of the logic and rhetoric stages of learning. That is, they are core studies in junior high and high school. Elementary school takes us back to the grammar stage of learning.

On the one hand, some families prefer to homeschool their children during the grammar stages. There are great resources and curriculum that is either designed for the home or adaptable to a homeschool setting. On the other hand, some children will have been schooled in methods and curricula that are not from the classical Christian model. In some cases, the schooling will be in other kinds of Christian schools or even public schools. Even if a student enters a classical Christian school for their senior year, there are benefits. I (Ben) began my transition to classical Christian education when I was nearly forty years old and an experienced teacher.

Elementary School

Classical Christian education goes with the grain of a child's learning style. God has given young children exceptional memory and learning skills. By the time children enter school, they have mastered language to an incredible degree. They are absorbing, assimilating, and learning at an amazing pace. Children memorize short songs, whole books that are read to them, and vast amounts of vocabulary.

Developmentally, they are ready to begin the more formal tasks of reading, writing, and arithmetic. There are numerous debates and lots of parental angst over when children read. However smart you might think your child is, there is some parent whose child is learning to read Homer in the original Greek while your baby is identifying letters in an alphabet book.

The key to reading success for your child involves several things. First, don't panic. Don't make your child run before he or she can walk or crawl. Second, at home focus on the fun and joy of books. It is more important that you and your child crawl up in a chair and read Dr. Suess than that they be able to identify letters. In the pre-school years, your child's personal reading abilities are not medical emergencies. Third, find a good school and talk with the administrator and lower elementary teachers. Trust the counsel of good teachers. Fourth, be aware that not all students have equal or even adequate reading abilities. The heavy reading schedules of a classical Christian education will not fit every student. Reading problems, whether visual or related to dyslexia or to other cognitive functions, hinder lots of children. You may have to get the advice and help of reading specialists. You might have to accept the fact that your child is severely challenged in the areas of visual learning. You might have to school your child yourself during most or all of the years of learning.

We say all these things about reading problems from this perspective: Colton and Ben are readers and the father of kids who are good readers (or who are growing into good readers). In a world where reading counts, we thrive. Ben once took a college class called "Fundamentals of Basketball." He made an A and was the top student in the class. The reason: the class was centered on studying a book, and only once did the student set foot in a gym. Athletically, mechanically, and musically, Ben may try, but he cannot succeed (Colton can personally testify to this). God gives different gifts to each of us. This implies that he also withholds from some that which He gives to others.

Typically, Classical Christian education in the elementary years produces good readers and book lovers. The goal is not to have children reading things beyond their level. I have never understood why some elementary teachers think *The Adventures of Huckleberry Finn* can be read in elementary school. Huck's friend Tom Sawyer had some swell adventures that makes for a great elementary read, but Huck's life experiences, though often simply told, call for a maturity that only later years can bring. *Huckleberry Finn* entails serious racial issues, ethical issues, violence, death, deceit, and parental abuse.

The way to determine if a children's book is good is simple. Do adults enjoy the book? Can mom and dad and the teacher read the book out loud and laugh at the story, delight in the rhymes, rhythms, and lyrical qualities, and rejoice when the wolves, dragons, and witches get their come-uppance? That's a good story.

Writing can also be mastered in the early years. Discussions of which method to use, when to transition from print to cursive, and what things to practice are again discussions to hold with the elementary teacher. It really gets back to this: a good teacher succeeds with even the worst of methods. Likewise, a great curriculum cannot make an inadequate teacher good. Teachers, at all levels, but particularly at the elementary level, are the curriculum.

Latin can begin rather early. Many schools begin around third grade. Latin vocabulary and, more important, Latin verb endings can be memorized, chanted, and sung. Memory skills are at their height during the grammar years. (Some classical Christian schools even boast that their first graders can read basic Bible verses in Greek! Our youngsters can do much more than we give them credit.)

History names and dates, parts of speech, lists of the states and their capitals, and numerous other lists can easily be drilled, memorized, chanted in unison, and made into songs as well. Elementary school must be loud. There is a joy to chanting in unison. There is joy in learning and singing. Elementary school should be bubbling over with those joys.

Some classical Christian schools opt not to have science in the elementary years. Of a truth, schools often get consumed with too many subjects. Some parents will react in horror. "How will my child ever be a chemist or a doctor if he doesn't have science in third grade"? We are not making the case for or against science in elementary school, and our school does have elementary science. But science will be learned, at whatever age, through reading and expressed through writing and verbal discussion.

Reading *The Cat in the Hat* and *The Cat in the Hat Comes Back* opens the door to the scientific method, to the world of possibilities and impossibilities, and the limitations and dangers of science and experimentation. Stories about the Wright Brothers and the Mayo brothers and stories from the Brothers Grimm are all worthy building blocks for future scientists. Frogs, flowers, and fall foliage are a rich curriculum for science. Learning and eating from the four major food groups, playing games focusing on coordination and kinetic skills, and singing will all train the mind for biology, chemistry, and physics in due time. No study of astronomy will surpass the wisdom of the little ditty "Twinkle, twinkle little star, how I wonder what you are."

The Goals of Grammar Education

Certainly, more could be discussed about the specifics of grammar, or elementary, school. Most of the questions need to be explored with an elementary principal and elementary teachers. As high school and middle school teachers, we stand in awe of what elementary teachers do. Don't just look at the curriculum guides and the textbooks; look at the teachers and their personalities, as reflected by their classrooms. There are some goals of grammar level education that need to be thought through.

First, elementary children absolutely must develop a love for learning. School must be described by children as fun. This does not mean that the child loves every moment of school and loves every assignment and subject. School is not a thirteen-year jail sentence. The key element in finding your school satisfying for your child is your home life. Cultivation of a good, godly, orderly, pleasant home will enable school to fulfill its partial mission.

A dysfunctional or near dysfunctional family with little or no church life and applied Christianity will most likely produce a student who cannot succeed in school. A Christian school is an extension of Christian living.

For children to love learning there must be a home that loves learning. This means that the family reads and reads together. This means that the family talks. This means that the family stops to look at flowers, fish jumping in a pond, rainbows, and clouds. This means that the family walks and talks the Bible. Deuteronomy 6:6–9, which you've seen multiple times by now in this book, expresses this well:

> And these words that I command you today shall be on your heart. You shall teach them diligently to your children, and shall talk of them when you sit in your house, and when you walk by the way, and when you lie down, and when you rise. You shall bind them as a sign on your hand, and they shall be as frontlets between your eyes. You shall write them on the doorposts of your house and on your gates.

You will spend far more money on your home, its furnishings, the food served there, and the atmosphere there than you ever will on tuition. That money should be well spent. This is not a book on family life, so we will not press on with this topic, but you need to read, talk with other Christian parents, and learn about Christian living in the home.

The love of learning, the fun of school, is not something separated from academic success. Children both delight to learn and, as sinners, rebel against the discipline of learning. The old saying about school was "Readin', Writin', and 'Rithmetic, taught to the tune of the hickory stick." There have been many teachers through the centuries who were embittered, insecure, mean-spirited task masters who made students hate school and learning. But they were teaching against the grain. Thank God for teachers who love learning, love children, and love God. The romance of the classroom is contagious when such a person is the teacher.

Second, parents must be very patient at evaluating their own child, especially during the elementary years. We all want our children to be the best and the brightest. We often envy those parents whose children far exceed ours. But most children's abilities fall into a broad spectrum of normal ranges. Smart children are just high on the normal range and slower children are often just low on the normal range. Most children and most people are average in most areas of life. School, by the way, focuses largely upon just a small part of the many areas of life.

There are many parents who assume their elementary age A+ student is bound to be a future Harvard graduate, a Nobel Prize winner, and both a doctor and a lawyer—all before they are twenty years old. There also those parents whose child is failing or struggling in school who believe their child is really bright, but is just not applying themselves to school. Often parents think some external factor, a previous teacher or educational program, is keeping the child from succeeding.

Be patient, parents, and be reserved in predicting the future. God is not as impressed with a straight A report card as we often are. God gives grace to the humble, and that is a difficult quest for many a gifted child (and an eager parent). A plodding, very average, often distracted, totally unorganized, and occasionally disruptive boy in fourth grade may become a surgeon (or even possibly a history teacher). An all A student may end up being an office bureaucrat doing mundane work efficiently.

God has not chosen to create a race or save by grace a group of super achievers, *magna cum laud* graduates, academically and socially elite movers and shakers, and MENSA members. A study of Jesus' apostles reveals quite a bit about the kind of people God most often uses. Thank God for the boy who studies Latin and calculus in school, and then says,

"Thank God that is over with," who then happily installs counter-tops for a career.

Young Winston Churchill could not talk without stuttering, and he thoroughly bombed Latin. He became a great orator whose speeches played a major role in helping Britain offset the Nazis in World War II. In 1953, this poor, stuttering student won the Nobel Prize for Literature. Young Albert Einstein flunked math. He is, of course, one of the most highly known and honored scientists of the twentieth century. James Fenimore Cooper got kicked out of college. According to his daughter, he hardly ever even wrote a letter. Then he became an incredibly prolific and successful author. A visiting preacher told a twelve year old boy named Billy to "Run along, little fellow, you'll never be a preacher."[1] Ask his son Franklin how his father turned out.

Second, things will happen to your children during the school years that you will not like. We wish our uniform policy included halos. We wish the children in a Christian school were all sweet, kind, loving, and generous both in the classroom and then in the real world, which for elementary kids means the playground. Every child brings things from home to buy, sell, and trade to other kids. By that, we mean that every child has some word they picked up, some movie they were allowed to watch, some shady, nasty, or questionable notion that they then eagerly spread to other children.

Sweet innocent children could get totally corrupted in a Christian school environment! But never fear, because there are no sweet, innocent children. A Christian education provides an atmosphere where God's grace and God's Word is taught, re-enforced, and applied. Shielding a child at home, even running off to the mountains, will not work. The gritty, slow, painful work of godly sanctification takes place not in a sheltered bubble, but in the home, the church, and Christian society, including Christian school playgrounds.

You may have heard this from other parents: "My child was such a good boy when he was younger. He was so sweet and loving. But now he has become disrespectful and he acts in ways that are upsetting."

---

[1] Nancy Gibbs and Michael Duffy, *The Preacher and the Presidents: Billy Graham in the White House* (New York: Center Street, 2007), 12.

Usually implied in this lament is something the school has done wrong. It is always other kids, the school atmosphere, and maybe even the teacher that turned some sweet precious angel into a junior high boy.

Moms, listen very closely. God gives us sweet, precious, cuddly little boys. But He does not want sweet, precious, cuddly men. (He wants men who can be sweet, precious, and cuddly, but only after they have subdued giants, dragons, and trolls.) We want men to resemble Sir Launcelot:

> "Thou wert the meekest man", says Sir Ector to the dead Launcelot. "Thou wert the meekest man that ever ate in hall among ladies; and thou wert the sternest knight to thy mortal foe that ever put spear in the rest."[2]

Through biological processes and cultural formation, your little dumpling will become or needs to become a chivalrous knight more akin to the High King Peter of Narnia than Justin Bieber. This is not to excuse disrespect or disobedience. This is not to allow profane language or ungodliness. The goal is Christian manhood. The goal is for mom not to say to her son, "Stay here by Mommy. There is a big bad Philistine out there." Rather, the goal is for her to say, "Get your slingshot, Dave. I want that ugly Philistine's head lopped off before breakfast."

The whole concept of manhood and masculinity is also a reminder that grammar school, which will rightfully be largely controlled by women, needs a cultural underpinning and outlet for masculinity. Male teachers and male presence is needed. Boys need to see strong men who love competition and books, grow (or want to grow) thick beards, and maybe even drive pick-up trucks. Students of both genders need men in their lives who are like Lancelot—stern yet gentle. In other words, students need to get around chivalrous men.

And when the teachers are mainly women, you need women who don't disdain male behavior (which is often near synonymous with male misbehavior). The test is really simple. Ask the teacher which child she would rather have in class: Tom Sawyer or his brother Sid Sawyer.

---

[2] C. S. Lewis, "The Necessity of Chivalry," quoting Sir Thomas Malory, *Le Morte D'Arthur* (1485), XXI, xii.

(If she hasn't read the book, give her an intense critical stare and then soften it to a look of pity.)

Sid Sawyer is a "perfect little student" and a sneak. No doubt, he got an A+ in conduct and probably snitched on the boys who broke school rules. Sid was a pansy, a wimp, a sycophant, and a very well-mannered, people pleaser. I would thoroughly dread having to spend any time around him in the classroom or otherwise.

What about Tom? Tom is a learner. He thinks creatively and imaginatively. He excels in social skills, doesn't judge by outward appearances, and steps up to lead. In the famous whitewashing the fence scene, Tom masters advertising and capitalism. In taking the blame for Becky Thatcher's misbehavior and taking the caning for it, he understands sacrifice for others. The escape to Sullivan's Island is about the greatest field trip ever. In witnessing his own funeral, he learns of mortality and love. In his confrontations with Injun Joe, he learns about truth, justice, oaths, and the great dangers of standing up for what are right.

Tom was bored by much of what he experienced in school, church, and life, but he was not broken into the harness of the mundane. Rather, every moment was a teachable moment and he was always a ready learner.

We're being a bit overgenerous to Tom, but let's get back to the point: boys in elementary school desperately need male teachers and women who understand the male temperament. Women teachers are most often strong in the areas of nurturing and detailing. Such a God-endowed demeanor is complimented by a man's risk taking and independence.

In the Grammar School, students need both men and women as teachers. The younger the student, the more motherly a figure is desperately needed. As the student becomes older, male teachers become more important to provide a fatherly figure in the classroom. God's design for manhood and womanhood and the exposure to both genders in the classroom is crucial for the spiritual and academic growth of your child.

Assignment for Chapter 16

Read 2 Timothy 3:10–16. Timothy had a great mentor in Paul. But he also had an incredible early education in holy living as presented by his mother and grandmother (2 Timothy 1:5). What does it mean to be made "wise for salvation" through the Holy Scriptures? What part does the Bible need to play in early childhood (elementary) education?

Scripture Memorization

2 Timothy 3:14–17:

> But as for you, continue in what you have learned and have firmly believed, knowing from whom you learned it and how from childhood you have been acquainted with the sacred writings, which are able to make you wise for salvation through faith in Christ Jesus. All Scripture is breathed out by God and profitable for teaching, for reproof, for correction, and for training in righteousness, that the man of God may be complete, equipped for every good work.

Recommended Reading Assignments

Anthony Esolen, *Ten Ways to Destroy the Imagination of Your Children* (Washington, DC: Regenery, 2013).

Chapter Seventeen

A Dreamy Conclusion

Another morning appointment had arrived. Once again, the parents walking in were greeted by a cheerful Mrs. Harrison. How does she manage to always either be or act so happy, I (Ben) thought. I glanced at the appointment schedule and noticed that the meeting was once again with Joseph and Alicia.

The cheer will end soon, I thought, as I positioned the Kleenex box close by for the tearful discussion that would soon follow.

To my surprise, Joseph sounded even merrier than Mrs. Harrison. "I'm doing great, like the Browning poem, 'The day's at the morn … God's in His heaven—All right with the world."

"You are doing great then," Mrs. Harrison answered. "And how about you, Alicia"?

"Great, the joy of the Lord is our strength," she answered cheerfully.

I was now wondering what medications Joseph and Alicia were taking. This was not at all what I had expected. They came into the office smiling. I stood, shook hands with both, and asked them to sit.

"So," I began slowly, "How are things at home? How are the children doing and the family as a whole"?

Joseph began, "Our children are a heritage from the Lord."

Alicia nodded and continued, "The fruit of the womb is a reward, like arrows in the hand of a warrior, so are the children of one's youth."

Joseph took her hand and added, "Happy is the man who has his quiver full of them: they shall not be ashamed, but shall speak with their enemies in the gate."

I began to feel awkward as Joseph and Alicia continued their gazes and smiles at each other.

"So, you have found Psalm 127 helpful for understanding your family."

They both nodded, but continued looking at each other.

"And how your children and school? Are you satisfied with them and the education they are receiving"?

Joseph answered, "As John Milton said, 'The end then of learning is to repair the ruins of our first parents by regaining to know God aright, and out of that knowledge to love Him, to imitate Him, to be like Him.'"

Alicia nodded and added, "It's like the Puritans, when they established Harvard College, just a few years after arriving in Massachusetts Colony. The rules of Harvard College said, 'Let every student be plainly instructed and earnestly pressed to consider well that the main end of his life and studies is to know God and Jesus Christ … and therefore to lay Christ in the bottom, as the only foundation of all sound knowledge and learning.'"

"But, Alicia," Joseph said, "Don't you think that Thomas Shepard, another Puritan, was saying pretty much the same thing when he told his son upon entering college, 'Remember the end of your life, which is coming back again to God, and fellowship with him'"?

"Certainly, Joseph, and Shepard also said to his son after he was in college, 'Remember that not only heavenly and spiritual and supernatural knowledge descends from God, but also all natural and human learning and abilities; and therefore pray much, not only for the one but also for the other."

"Alicia, I totally agree about that. All knowledge is from God. As John Calvin said, 'All men that have said anything that is true and just, we ought not to reject it; for it has come from God."

And on it went, with more quotes from Augustine, C. S. Lewis, Dorothy Sayers, J. R. R. Tolkien, Martin Luther, Douglas Wilson, George Grant, and more. Snippets from Plato, Latin phrases, warnings about logical fallacies, and the like were bandied back and forth. My mind was whirling and swirling around with what sounded like a vigorous argument at moments as what Mortimer Adler called "the Great Conversation" was taking place in my office.

When there was finally a pause in their talk, I said, "I think you both have made great progress. Not only are you fully behind classical Christian education for your children, but you seem to have embraced it yourselves."

Joseph answered, "As C. S. Lewis in his essay 'Education in Wartime,' said, 'If we let ourselves, we shall always be waiting for some distraction or other to end before we can really get down to our work. The only people who achieve much are those who want knowledge so badly that they seek it while the conditions are still unfavorable. Favorable conditions never come.'"

Alicia then added, "We were like the man William Wilberforce described as being in need of 'the chastening hand of a sound classical education.'"

And once again, they started. Quotes, poems, desires ("When can we start reading *The Brothers Karamazov*?"), and even minor arguments ("No, *Pride and Prejudice* is Jane Austen's greatest work, although *Emma* comes as a close second").

Mrs. Harrison then stepped into the office. "Your next appointment has arrived. It is the Smith's. They don't look too happy."

Joseph and Alicia stood up to leave, still beaming.

"Joseph, Alicia, would you two mind waiting? I would like to introduce you to the Smith's. Their children have recently enrolled in our school."

Assignment for Chapter 16

Read Ecclesiastes 12. The chapter is rich in content about education. The warnings about fearing God in youth lead to lots of implications for education and child raising.

Scripture Memorization

Ecclesiastes 12:9–10:

> Besides being wise, the Preacher also taught the people knowledge, weighing and studying and arranging many proverbs with great care. The Preacher sought to find words of delight, and uprightly he wrote words of truth.

Recommended Reading Assignments

Leland Ryken, "The Student's Calling" in *The Liberal Arts for the Christian Life*, Jeffrey C. Davis and Philip G. Ryken, eds. (Wheaton, IL: Crossway, 2012).

APPENDIX 1

THE LOST TOOLS OF LEARNING[1]

That I, whose experience of teaching is extremely limited, and whose life of recent years has been almost wholly out of touch with educational circles, should presume to discuss education is a matter, surely, that calls for no apology. It is a kind of behaviour to which the present climate of opinion is wholly favourable. Bishops air their opinions about economics; biologists, about metaphysics; celibates, about matrimony; inorganic chemists about theology; the most irrelevant people are appointed to highly-technical ministries; and plain, blunt men write to the papers to say that Epstein and Picasso do not know how to draw. Up to a certain point, and provided that the criticisms are made with a reasonable modesty, these activities are commendable. Too much specialisation is not a good thing. There is also one excellent reason why the veriest amateur may feel entitled to have an opinion about education. For if we are not all professional teachers, we have all, at some time or other, been taught. Even if we learnt nothing—perhaps in particular if we learnt nothing—our contribution to the discussion may have a potential value.

Without apology, then, I will begin. But since much that I have to say is highly controversial, it will be pleasant to start with a proposition with which, I feel confident, all teachers will cordially agree; and that is, that they all work much too hard and have far too many things to do. One has only to look at any school or examination syllabus to see that it is cluttered up with a great variety of exhausting subjects which they are called upon to teach, and the teaching of which sadly interferes with what every thoughtful mind will allow to be their proper duties, such as

[1] The complete text of Dorothy L. Sayers, *The Lost Tools of Learning* is reprinted in this appendix. Miss Sayers' article is in the public domain. She first gave this lecture in 1947 at Oxford University.

distributing milk, supervising meals, taking cloak-room duty, weighing and measuring pupils, keeping their eyes open for incipient mumps, measles and chicken-pox, making out lists, escorting parties round the Victoria and Albert Museum, filling up forms, interviewing parents, and devising end-of-term reports which shall combine a deep veneration for truth with a tender respect for the feelings of all concerned.

Upon these really important duties I will not enlarge. I propose only to deal with the subject of teaching, properly so-called. I want to inquire whether, amid all the multitudinous subjects which figure in the syllabuses, we are really teaching the right things in the right way; and whether, by teaching fewer things, differently, we might not succeed in "shedding the load" (as the fashionable phrase goes) and, at the same time, producing a better result.

This prospect need arouse neither hope nor alarm. It is in the highest degree improbable that the reforms I propose will ever be carried into effect. Neither the parents, nor the training colleges, nor the examination boards, nor the boards of governors, nor the Ministry of Education would countenance them for a moment. For they amount to this: that if we are to produce a society of educated people, fitted to preserve their intellectual freedom amid the complex pressures of our modern society, we must turn back the wheel of progress some four or five hundred years, to the point at which education began to lose sight of its true object, towards the end of the Middle Ages.

Before you dismiss me with the appropriate phrase—reactionary, romantic, mediaevalist, *laudator temporis acti*, or whatever tag comes first to hand—I will ask you to consider one or two miscellaneous questions that hang about at the back, perhaps, of all our minds, and occasionally pop out to worry us.

When we think about the remarkably early age at which the young men went up to the University in, let us say, Tudor times, and thereafter were held fit to assume responsibility for the conduct of their own affairs, are we altogether comfortable about that artificial prolongation of intellectual childhood and adolescence into the years of physical maturity which is so marked in our own day? To postpone the acceptance of responsibility to a late date brings with it a number of psychological complications which, while they may interest the psychiatrist, are scarcely beneficial either to the individual or to society. The stock argument in favour of postponing the school leaving-age and prolonging the period of education generally is that there is now so much more to learn than there was in the Middle Ages. This is partly true, but not wholly. The modern boy and girl are certainly taught more subjects—but does that always mean that they are actually more learned and know more? That is the very point which we are going to consider.

Has it ever struck you as odd, or unfortunate, that today, when the proportion of literacy throughout Western Europe is higher than it has ever been, people should have become susceptible to the influence of advertisement and mass-propaganda to an extent hitherto unheard-of and unimagined? Do you put this down to the mere mechanical fact that the press and the radio and so on have made propaganda much easier to distribute over a wide area? Or do you sometimes have an uneasy suspicion that the product of modern educational methods is less good than he or she might be at disentangling fact from opinion and the proven from the plausible?

Have you ever, in listening to a debate among adult and presumably responsible people, been fretted by the extraordinary inability of the average debater to speak to the question, or to meet and refute the arguments of speakers on the other side? Or have you ever pondered upon the extremely high incidence of irrelevant matter which crops up at committee meetings, and upon the very great rarity of persons capable of acting as chairmen of committees? And when you think of this, and think that most of our public affairs are settled by debates and committees, have you ever felt a certain sinking of the heart?

Have you ever followed a discussion in the newspapers or elsewhere and noticed how frequently writers fail to define the terms they use? Or how often, if one man does define his terms, another will assume in his reply that he was using the terms in precisely the opposite sense to that in which he has already defined them?

Have you ever been faintly troubled by the amount of slipshod syntax going about? And if so, are you troubled because it is inelegant or because it may lead to dangerous misunderstanding?

Do you ever find that young people, when they have left school, not only forget most of what they have learnt (that is only to be expected) but forget also, or betray that they have never really known, how to tackle a new subject for themselves? Are you often bothered by coming across grown-up men and women who seem unable to distinguish between a book that is sound, scholarly and properly documented, and one that is to any trained eye, very conspicuously none of these things? Or who cannot handle a library catalogue? Or who, when faced with a book of reference, betray a curious inability to extract from it the passages relevant to the particular question which interests them?

Do you often come across people for whom, all their lives, a "subject" remains a "subject," divided by water-tight bulkheads from all other "subjects," so that they experience very great difficulty in making an immediate mental connection between, let us say, algebra and detective fiction, sewage disposal and the price of salmon, cellulose and the distribution of rainfall—or, more generally, between such spheres of knowledge as philosophy and economics, or chemistry and art?

Are you occasionally perturbed by the things written by adult men and women for adult men and women to read? Here, for instance, is a quotation from an evening paper. It refers to the visit of an Indian girl to this country:

> Miss Bhosle has a perfect command of English ("Oh, gosh," she said once), and a marked enthusiasm for London.

Well, we may all talk nonsense in a moment of inattention. It is more alarming when we find a well-known biologist writing in a weekly paper to the effect that: "It is an argument against the existence of a Creator" (I think he put it more strongly; but since I have, most unfortunately, mislaid the reference, I will put his claim at its lowest)—"an argument against the existence of a Creator that the same kind of variations which are produced by natural selection can be produced at will by stockbreeders." One might feel tempted to say that it is rather an argument *for* the existence of a Creator. Actually, of course, it is neither: all it proves is that the same material causes (re-combination of the chromosomes by cross-breeding and so forth) are sufficient to account for all observed variations—just as the various combinations of the same 13 semitones are materially sufficient to account for Beethoven's

Moonlight Sonata and the noise the cat makes by walking on the keys. But the cat's performance neither proves nor disproves the existence of Beethoven; and all that is proved by the biologist's argument is that he was unable to distinguish between a material and a final cause.

Here is a sentence from no less academic a source than a front-page article in the *Times Literary Supplement*:

> The Frenchman, Alfred Epinas, pointed out that certain species (*e.g.*, ants and wasps) can only face the horrors of life and death in association.

I do not know what the Frenchman actually did say: what the Englishman says he said is patently meaningless. We cannot know whether life holds any horror for the ant, nor in what sense the isolated wasp which you kill upon the window-pane can be said to "face" or not to “face” the horrors of death. The subject of the article is mass-behaviour in *man*; and the human motives have been unobtrusively transferred from the main proposition to the supporting instance. Thus the argument, in effect, assumes what it sets out to prove—a fact which would become immediately apparent if it were presented in a formal syllogism. This is only a small and haphazard example of a vice which pervades whole books—particularly books written by men of science on metaphysical subjects.

Another quotation from the same issue of the T.L.S. comes in fittingly here to wind up this random collection of disquieting thoughts—this time from a review of Sir Richard Livingstone's *Some Tasks for Education*:

> More than once the reader is reminded of the value of an intensive study of at least one subject, so as to learn "the meaning of knowledge" and what precision and persistence is needed to attain it. Yet there is elsewhere full recognition of the distressing fact that a man may be master in one field and show no better judgment than his neighbour anywhere else; he remembers what he has learnt, but forgets altogether how he learned it.

I would draw your attention particularly to that last sentence, which offers an explanation of what the writer rightly calls the "distressing fact" that the intellectual skills bestowed upon us by our education are not readily transferable to subjects other than those in which we acquired them: "he remembers what he has learnt, but forgets altogether how he learned it."

Is not the great defect of our education today—a defect traceable through all the disquieting symptoms of trouble that I have mentioned--that although we often succeed in teaching our pupils "subjects," we fail lamentably on the whole in teaching them how to think? They learn everything, except the art of learning. It is as though we had taught a child, mechanically and by rule of thumb, to play *The Harmonious Blacksmith* upon the piano, but had never taught him the scale or how to read music; so that, having memorised *The Harmonious Blacksmith*, he still had not the faintest notion how to proceed from that to tackle *The Last Rose of Summer*. Why do I say, "As though"? In certain of the arts and crafts we sometimes do precisely this—requiring a child to "express himself" in paint before we teach him how to handle the colours and the brush. There is a school of thought which believes this to be the right way to set about the job. But observe—it is not the way in which a trained craftsman will go about to teach himself a new medium. *He*, having learned by experience the best way to economise labour and take the thing by the right end, will start off by doodling about on an odd piece of material, in order to "give himself the feel of the tool."

Let us now look at the mediaeval scheme of education—the syllabus of the Schools. It does not matter, for the moment, whether it was devised for small children or for older students; or how long people were supposed to take over it. What matters is the light it throws upon what the men of the Middle Ages supposed to be the object and the right order of the educative process.

The syllabus was divided into two parts; the Trivium and Quadrivium. The second part—the Quadrivium—consisted of "subjects," and need not for the moment concern us. The interesting thing for us is the composition of the Trivium, which preceded the Quadrivium and was the preliminary discipline for it. It consisted of three parts: Grammar, Dialectic, and Rhetoric, in that order.

Now the first thing we notice is that two at any rate of these "subjects" are not what we should call "subjects" at all: they are only methods of dealing with subjects. Grammar, indeed, is a "subject" in the sense that it does mean definitely learning a language—at that period it meant learning Latin. But language itself is simply the medium in which thought is expressed. The whole of the Trivium was, in fact, intended to teach the pupil the proper use of the tools of learning, before he began to apply them to "subjects" at all. First, he learned a language; not just how to order a meal in a foreign language, but the structure of language—a language, and hence of language itself—what it was, how it was put together and how it worked. Secondly, he learned how to use language: how to define his terms and make accurate statements; how to construct an argument and how to detect fallacies in argument (his own arguments and other people's). Dialectic, that is to say, embraced Logic and Disputation. Thirdly, he learned to express himself in language; how to say what he had to say elegantly and persuasively. At this point, any tendency to express himself windily or to use his eloquence so as to make the worse appear the better reason would, no doubt, be restrained by his previous teaching in Dialectic. If not, his teacher and his fellow-pupils, trained along the same lines, would be quick to point out where he was wrong; for it was they whom he had to seek to persuade. At the end of his course, he was required to compose a thesis upon some theme set by his masters or chosen by himself, and afterwards to defend his thesis against the criticism of the faculty. By this time he would have learned—or woe betide him—not merely to write an essay on paper, but to speak audibly and intelligibly from a platform, and to use his wits quickly when heckled. The heckling, moreover, would not consist solely of offensive personalities or of irrelevant queries about what Julius Caesar said in 55 B.C.—though no doubt mediaeval dialectic was enlivened in practice by plenty of such primitive repartee. But there would also be questions, cogent and shrewd, from those who had already run the gauntlet of debate, or were making ready to run it.

It is, of course, quite true that bits and pieces of the mediaeval tradition still linger, or have been revived, in the ordinary school syllabus of today. Some knowledge of grammar is still required when learning a foreign language—perhaps I should say, "is again required"; for during my own lifetime we passed through a phase when the teaching of declensions and conjugations was considered rather reprehensible, and it was considered better to pick these things up as we went along. School debating societies flourish; essays are written; the necessity for "self-expression" is stressed, and perhaps even over-stressed. But these activities are cultivated more or less in detachment, as belonging to the special subjects in which they are pigeon-holed rather than as forming one coherent scheme of mental training to which all "subjects" stand in a subordinate relation. "Grammar" belongs especially to the "subject" of foreign languages, and essay-writing to the "subject" called "English"; while Dialectic has become almost entirely divorced from the rest of the curriculum, and is frequently practised unsystematically and out of school-hours as a separate exercise, only very loosely related to the main business of learning. Taken by and large, the great difference of emphasis between the two conceptions holds good: modern education concentrates on *teaching subjects*, leaving the method of thinking, arguing and expressing one's conclusions to be picked up by the scholar as he goes along; mediaeval education concentrated on first *forging and learning to handle the tools of learning*, using whatever subject came handy as a piece of material on which to doodle until the use of the tool became second nature.

"Subjects" of some kind there must be, of course. One cannot learn the use of a tool by merely waving it in the air; neither can one learn the theory of grammar without learning an actual language, or learn to argue and orate without speaking about something in particular. The debating subjects of the Middle Ages were drawn largely from Theology, or from the Ethics and History of Antiquity. Often, indeed, they became stereotyped, especially towards the end of the period, and the far-fetched and wire-drawn absurdities of scholastic argument fretted Milton and provide food for merriment even to this day. Whether they were in themselves any more hackneyed and trivial than the usual subjects set nowadays for "essay-writing" I should not like to say: we may ourselves grow a little weary of "A Day in my Holidays," "What I should like to Do when I Leave School," and all the rest of it. But most of the merriment is misplaced, because the aim and object of the debating thesis has by now been lost sight of. A glib speaker in the Brains Trust once entertained his audience (and reduced the late Charles Williams to helpless rage) by asserting that in the Middle Ages it was a matter of faith to know how many archangels could dance on the point of a needle. I need not say, I hope, that it never was a "matter of faith"; it was simply a debating exercise, whose set subject was the nature of angelic substance: were angels material, and if so, did they occupy space? The answer usually adjudged correct is, I believe, that angels are pure intelligences; not material, but limited, so that they may have location in space but not extension. An analogy might be drawn from human thought, which is similarly non-material and similarly limited. Thus, if your thought is concentrated upon one thing—say, the point of a needle—it is located there in the sense that it is not elsewhere; but although it is "there," it occupies no space there, and there is nothing to prevent an infinite number of different people's thoughts being concentrated upon the same needle-point at the same time. The proper subject of the argument is thus seen to be the distinction between location and extension in space; the matter on which the argument is exercised happens to be the nature of angels (although, as we have seen, it might equally well have been something else); the practical lesson to be drawn from the argument is not to use words like "there" in a loose and unscientific way, without specifying whether you mean "located there" or "occupying space there." Scorn in plenty has been poured out upon the mediaeval passion for hair-splitting: but when we look at the shameless abuse made, in print and on the platform, of controversial expressions with shifting and ambiguous connotations, we may feel it in our hearts to wish that every reader and hearer had been so defensively armoured by his education as to be able to cry: *Distinguo.*

For we let our young men and women go out unarmed, in a day when armour was never so necessary. By teaching them all to read, we have left them at the mercy of the printed word. By the invention of the film and the radio, we have made certain that no aversion to reading shall secure them from the incessant battery of words, words, words. They do not know what the words mean; they do not know how to ward them off or blunt their edge or fling them back; they are a prey to words in their emotions instead of being the masters of them in their intellects.

We who were scandalised in 1940 when men were sent to fight armoured tanks with rifles, are not scandalised when young men and women are sent into the world to fight massed propaganda with a smattering of "subjects"; and when whole classes and whole nations become hypnotised by the arts of the spell-binder, we have the impudence to be astonished. We dole out lip-service to the importance of education—lip-service and, just occasionally, a little grant of money; we postpone the school leaving-age, and plan to build bigger and better schools; the teachers slave conscientiously in and out of school-hours, till responsibility becomes a burden and a nightmare; and yet, as I believe, all this devoted effort is largely frustrated, because we have lost the tools of learning, and in their absence can only make a botched and piecemeal job of it.

What, then, are we to do? We cannot go back to the Middle Ages. That is a cry to which we have become accustomed. We cannot go back--or can we? *Distinguo.* I should like every term in that proposition defined. Does "Go back" mean a retrogression in time, or the revision of an error? The first is clearly impossible *per se*; the second is a thing which wise men do every day. "Cannot"—does this mean that our behaviour is determined by some irreversible cosmic mechanism, or merely that such an action would be very difficult in view of the opposition it would provoke? "The Middle Ages"—obviously the 20th century is not and cannot be the 14th; but if "the Middle Ages" is, in this context, simply a picturesque phrase denoting a particular educational theory, there seems to be no *a priori* reason why we should not "go back" to it—with modifications—as we have already "gone back," with modifications, to, let us say, the idea of playing Shakespeare's plays as he wrote them, and not in the "modernized" versions of Cibber and Garrick, which once seemed to be the latest thing in theatrical progress.

Let us amuse ourselves by imagining that such progressive retrogression is possible. Let us make a clean sweep of all educational authorities, and furnish ourselves with a nice little school of boys and girls whom we may experimentally equip for the intellectual conflict along lines chosen by ourselves. We will endow them with exceptionally docile parents; we will staff our school with teachers who are themselves perfectly familiar with the aims and methods of the Trivium; we will have our buildings and staff large enough to allow our classes to be small enough for adequate handling; and we will postulate a Board of Examiners willing and qualified to test the products we turn out. Thus prepared, we will attempt to sketch out a syllabus—a modern Trivium "with modifications"; and we will see where we get to.

But first: what age shall the children be? Well, if one is to educate them on novel lines, it will be better that they should have nothing to unlearn; besides, one cannot begin a good thing too early, and the Trivium is by its nature not learning, but a preparation for learning. We will, therefore, "catch 'em young," requiring only of our pupils that they shall be able to read, write and cipher.

My views about child-psychology are, I admit, neither orthodox nor enlightened. Looking back upon myself (since I am the child I know best and the only child I can pretend to know from inside) I recognise in myself three stages of development. These, in a rough-and-ready fashion, I will call the Poll-parrot, the Pert, and the Poetic—the latter coinciding, approximately, with the onset of puberty. The Poll-parrot stage is the one in which learning by heart is easy and, on the whole, pleasurable; whereas reasoning is difficult and, on the whole, little relished. At this age, one readily memorises the shapes and appearances of things; one likes to recite the number-plates of cars; one rejoices in the chanting of rhymes and the rumble and thunder of unintelligible polysyllables; one enjoys the mere accumulation of things. The Pert Age, which follows upon this (and, naturally, overlaps it to some extent) is only too familiar to all who have to do with children: it is characterised by contradicting, answering-back, liking to "catch people out" (especially one's elders) and in the propounding of conundrums (especially the kind with a nasty verbal catch in them). Its nuisance-value is extremely high. It usually sets in about the Lower Fourth. The Poetic Age is popularly known as the "difficult" age. It is self-centred; it yearns to express itself; it rather specialises in being misunderstood; it is restless and tries to achieve independence; and, with good luck and good guidance, it should show the beginnings of creativeness, a reaching-out towards a synthesis of what it already knows, and a deliberate eagerness to know and do some one thing in preference to all others. Now it seems to me that the lay-out of the Trivium adapts itself with a singular appropriateness to these three ages: Grammar to the Poll-parrot, Dialectic to the Pert, and Rhetoric to the Poetic age.

Let us begin, then, with Grammar. This, in practice, means the grammar of some language in particular; and it must be an inflected language. The grammatical structure of an uninflected language is far too analytical to be tackled by any one without previous practice in Dialectic. Moreover, the inflected languages interpret the uninflected, whereas the uninflected are of little use in interpreting the inflected. I will say at once, quite firmly, that the best grounding for education is the Latin grammar. I say this, not because Latin is traditional and mediaeval, but simply because even a rudimentary knowledge of Latin cuts down the labour and pains of learning almost any other subject by at least fifty per cent. It is the key to the vocabulary and structure of all the Romance languages and to the structure of all the Teutonic languages, as well as to the technical vocabulary of all the sciences and to the literature of the entire Mediterranean civilisation, together with all its historical documents. Those whose pedantic preference for a living language persuades them to deprive their pupils of all these advantages might substitute Russian, whose grammar is still more primitive. (The verb is complicated by a number of "aspects"—and I rather fancy that it enjoys three complete voices and a couple of extra aorists—but I may be thinking of Basque or Sanskrit.) Russian is, of course, helpful with the other Slav dialects. There is something also to be said for Classical Greek. But my own choice is Latin. Having thus pleased the Classicists among you, I will proceed to horrify them by adding that I do not think it either wise or necessary to cramp the ordinary pupil upon the Procrustean bed of the Augustan age, with its highly elaborate and artificial verse-forms and oratory. The post-classical and mediaeval Latin, which was a living language down to the end of the Renaissance, is easier and in some ways livelier, both in syntax and rhythm; and a study of it helps to dispel the widespread notion that learning and literature came to a full-stop when Christ was born and only woke up again at the Dissolution of the Monasteries.

However, I am running ahead too fast. We are still in the grammatical stage. Latin should be begun as early as possible—at a time when inflected speech seems no more astonishing than any other phenomenon in an astonishing world; and when the chanting of "amo, amas, amat" is as ritually agreeable to the feelings as the chanting of "eeny, meeny, miney, mo."

During this age we must, of course, exercise the mind on other things besides Latin grammar. Observation and memory are the faculties most lively at this period; and if we are to learn a contemporary foreign language we should begin now, before the facial and mental muscles become rebellious to strange intonations. Spoken French or German can be practised alongside the grammatical discipline of the Latin.

In *English*, verse and prose can be learned by heart, and the pupil's memory should be stored with stories of every kind—classical myth, European legend, and so forth. I do not think that the Classical stories and masterpieces of ancient literature should be made the vile bodies on which to practise the technics of Grammar—that was a fault of mediaeval education which we need not perpetuate. The stories can be enjoyed and remembered in English, and related to their origin at a subsequent stage. Recitation aloud should be practiced—individually or in chorus; for we must not forget that we are laying the ground work for Disputation and Rhetoric.

The grammar of *History* should consist, I think, of dates, events, anecdotes and personalities. A set of dates to which one can peg all later historical knowledge is of enormous help later on in establishing the perspective of history. It does not greatly matter *which* dates: those of the Kings of England will do very nicely, provided that they are accompanied by pictures of costume, architecture, and other "every-day things," so that the mere mention of a date calls up a strong visual presentment of the whole period.

Geography will similarly be presented in its factual aspect, with maps, natural features and visual presentment of customs, costumes, flora, fauna and so on; and I believe myself that the discredited and old-fashioned memorising of a few capital cities, rivers, mountain ranges, etc., does no harm. Stamp-collecting may be encouraged.

Science, in the Poll-parrot period, arranges itself naturally and easily round collections—he identifying and naming of specimens and, in general, the kind of thing that used to be called "natural history," or, still more charmingly, “natural philosophy.” To know the names and properties of things is, at this age, a satisfaction in itself; to recognise a devil’s coach-horse at sight, and assure one’s foolish elders that, in spite of its appearance, it does not sting; to be able to pick out Cassiopeia and the Pleiades, and possibly even to know who Cassiopeia and the Pleiades were; to be aware that a whale is not a fish, and a bat not a bird--all these things give a pleasant sensation of superiority; while to know a ring-snake from an adder or a poisonous from an edible toadstool is a kind of knowledge that has also a practical value.

The grammar of *Mathematics* begins, of course, with the multiplication table, which, if not learnt now will never be learnt with pleasure; and with the recognition of geometrical shapes and the grouping of numbers. These exercises lead naturally to the doing of simple sums in arithmetic; and if the pupil shows a bent that way, a facility acquired at this stage is all to the good. More complicated mathematical processes may, and perhaps should, be postponed, for reasons which will presently appear.

So far (except, of course, for the Latin), our curriculum contains nothing that departs very far from common practice. The difference will be felt rather in the attitude of the teachers, who must look upon all these activities less as “subjects” in themselves than as a gathering-together of *material* for use in the next part of the Trivium. What that material actually is, is only of secondary importance; but it is as well that anything and everything which can usefully be committed to memory should be memorised at this period, whether it is immediately intelligible or not. The modern tendency is to try and force rational explanations on a child’s mind at too early an age. Intelligent questions, spontaneously asked, should, of course, receive an immediate and rational answer; but it is a great mistake to suppose that a child cannot readily enjoy and remember things that are beyond its power to analyse—particularly if those things have a strong imaginative appeal (as, for example, *Kubla Khan*), an attractive jingle (like some of the memory-rhymes for Latin genders), or an abundance of rich, resounding polysyllables (like the *Quicunque Vult*).

This reminds me of the Grammar of *Theology*. I shall add it to the curriculum, because Theology is the mistress-science, without which the whole educational structure will necessarily lack its final synthesis. Those who disagree about this will remain content to leave their pupils' education still full of loose ends. This will matter rather less than it might, since by the time that the tools of learning have been forged the student will be able to tackle Theology for himself, and will probably insist upon doing so and making sense of it. Still, it is as well to have this matter also handy and ready for the reason to work upon. At the grammatical age, therefore, we should become acquainted with the story of God and Man in outline—*i.e.*, the Old and New Testament presented as parts of a single narrative of Creation, Rebellion and Redemption—and also with "the Creed, the Lord's Prayer and the Ten Commandments." At this stage, it does not matter nearly so much that these things should be fully understood as that they should be known and remembered. Remember, it is material that we are collecting.

It is difficult to say at what age, precisely, we should pass from the first to the second part of the Trivium. Generally speaking, the answer is: so soon as the pupil shows himself disposed to Pertness and interminable argument (or, as a schoolmaster correspondent of mine more elegantly puts it: "When the capacity for abstract thought begins to manifest itself"). For as, in the first part, the master-faculties are Observation and Memory, so in the second, the master-faculty is the Discursive Reason. In the first, the exercise to which the rest of the material was, as it were, keyed, was the Latin Grammar; in the second the key-exercise will be Formal Logic. It is here that our curriculum shows its first sharp divergence from modern standards. The disrepute into which Formal Logic has fallen is entirely unjustified; and its neglect is the root cause of nearly all those disquieting symptoms which we have noted in the modern intellectual constitution. Logic has been discredited, partly because we have fallen into a habit of supposing that we are conditioned almost entirely by the intuitive and the unconscious. There is no time now to argue whether this is true; I will content myself with observing that to neglect the proper training of the reason is the best possible way to make it true, and to ensure the supremacy of the intuitive, irrational and unconscious elements in our make-up. A secondary cause for the disfavour into which Formal Logic has fallen is the belief that it is entirely based upon universal assumptions that are either unprovable or tautological. This is not true. Not all universal propositions are of this kind. But even if they were, it would make no difference, since every syllogism whose major premise is in the form "All A is B" can be recast in hypothetical form. Logic is the art of arguing correctly: "If A, then B"; the method is not invalidated by the hypothetical character of A. Indeed, the practical utility of Formal Logic to-day lies not so much in the establishment of positive conclusions as in the prompt detection and exposure of invalid inference.

Let us now quickly review our material and see how it is to be related to Dialectic. On the *Language* side, we shall now have our Vocabulary and Morphology at our finger-tips; henceforward we can concentrate more particularly on Syntax and Analysis (*i.e.*, the logical construction of speech) and the history of Language (*i.e.*, how we came to arrange our speech as we do in order to convey our thoughts).

Our Reading will proceed from narrative and lyric to essays, argument and criticism, and the pupil will learn to try his own hand at writing this kind of thing. Many lessons—on whatever subject—will take the form of debates; and the place of individual or choral recitation will be taken by dramatic performances, with special attention to plays in which an argument is stated in dramatic form.

Mathematics—Algebra, Geometry, and the more advanced kind of Arithmetic—will now enter into the syllabus and take its place as what it really is: not a separate "subject" but a sub-department of Logic. It is neither more nor less than the rule of the syllogism in its particular application to number and measurement, and should be taught as such, instead of being, for some, a dark mystery, and for others, a special revelation, neither illuminating nor illuminated by any other part of knowledge.

History, aided by a simple system of ethics derived from the Grammar of Theology, will provide much suitable material for discussion; Was the behaviour of this statesman justified? What was the effect of such an enactment? What are the arguments for and against this or that form of government? We shall thus get an introduction to Constitutional History—a subject meaningless to the young child, but of absorbing interest to those who are prepared to argue and debate. *Theology* itself will furnish material for argument about conduct and morals; and should have its scope extended by a simplified course of dogmatic theology (i.e., the rational structure of Christian thought), clarifying the relations between the dogma and the ethics, and lending itself to that application of ethical principles in particular instances which is properly called casuistry. *Geography* and the *Sciences* will all likewise provide material for Dialectic.

But above all, we must not neglect the material which is so abundant in the pupils' own daily life. There is a delightful passage in Leslie Paul's *The Living Hedge* which tells how a number of small boys enjoyed themselves for days arguing about an extraordinary shower of rain which had fallen in their town—a shower so localised that it left one half of the main street wet and the other dry. Could one, they argued, properly say that it had rained that day on or over the town or only in the town? How many drops of water were required to constitute rain? and so on. Argument about this led on to a host of similar problems about rest and motion, sleep and waking, *est* and *non est*, and the infinitesimal division of time. The whole passage is an admirable example of the spontaneous development of the ratiocinative faculty and the natural and proper thirst of the awakening reason for definition of terms and exactness of statement. All events are food for such an appetite. An umpire's decision; the degree to which one may transgress the spirit of a regulation without being trapped by the letter; on such questions as these, children are born casuists, and their natural propensity only needs to be developed and trained—and, especially, brought into an intelligible relationship with events in the grown-up world. The newspapers are full of good material for such exercises: legal decisions, on the one hand, in cases where the cause at issue is not too abstruse; on the other, fallacious reasoning and muddle-headed argument, with which the correspondence columns of certain papers one could name are abundantly stocked.

Wherever the matter for Dialectic is found, it is, of course, highly important that attention should be focused upon the beauty and economy of a fine demonstration or a well-turned argument, lest veneration should wholly die. Criticism must not be merely destructive; though at the same time both teacher and pupils must be ready to detect fallacy, slipshod reasoning, ambiguity, irrelevance and redundancy, and to pounce upon them like rats.

This is the moment when precis-writing may be usefully undertaken; together with such exercises as the writing of an essay, and the reduction of it, when written, by 25 or 50 per cent.

It will, doubtless, be objected that to encourage young persons at the Pert Age to browbeat, correct and argue with their elders will render them perfectly intolerable. My answer is that children of that age are intolerable anyhow; and that their natural argumentativeness may just as well be canalised to good purpose as allowed to run away into the sands. It may, indeed, be rather less obtrusive at home if it is disciplined in school; and, anyhow, elders who have abandoned the wholesome principle that children should be seen and not heard have no one to blame but themselves. The teachers, to be sure, will have to mind their step, or they may get more than they bargained for. All children sit in judgment on their masters; and if the Chaplain's sermon or the Headmistress's annual Speech-day address should by any chance afford an opening for the point of the critical wedge, that wedge will go home the more forcibly under the weight of the Dialectical hammer, wielded by a practised hand. That is why I said that the teachers themselves would need to undergo the discipline of the Trivium before they set out to impose it on their charges.

Once again: the contents of the syllabus at this stage may be anything you like. The "subjects" supply material; but they are all to be regarded as mere grist for the mental mill to work upon. The pupils should be encouraged to go and forage for their own information, and so guided towards the proper use of libraries and books of reference, and shown how to tell which sources are authoritative and which are not.

Towards the close of this stage, the pupils will probably be beginning to discover for themselves that their knowledge and experience are insufficient, and that their trained intelligences need a great deal more material to chew upon. The imagination—usually dormant during the Pert age—will re-awaken, and prompt them to suspect the limitations of logic and reason. This means that they are passing into the Poetic age and are ready to embark on the study of Rhetoric. The doors of the storehouse of knowledge should now be thrown open for them to browse about as they will. The things once learned by rote will be seen in new contexts; the things once coldly analysed can now be brought together to form a new synthesis; here and there a sudden insight will bring about that most exciting of all discoveries: the realisation that a truism is true.

It is difficult to map out any general syllabus for the study of Rhetoric: a certain freedom is demanded. In literature, appreciation should be again allowed to take the lead over destructive criticism; and self-expression in writing can go forward, with its tools now sharpened to cut clean and observe proportion. Any child that already shows a disposition to specialise should be given his head: for, when the use of the tools has been well and truly learned it is available for any study whatever. It would be well, I think, that each pupil should learn to do one, or two, subjects really well, while taking a few classes in subsidiary subjects so as to keep his mind open to the inter-relations of all knowledge. Indeed, at this stage, our difficulty will be to keep "subjects" apart; for as Dialectic will have shown all branches of learning to be inter-related, so Rhetoric will tend to show that all knowledge is one. To show this, and show why it is so, is pre-eminently the task of the Mistress-science. But whether Theology is studied or not, we should at least insist that children who seem inclined to specialise on the mathematical and scientific side should be obliged to attend some lessons in the Humanities and *vice versa*. At this stage also, the Latin Grammar, having done its work, may be dropped for those who prefer to carry on their language studies on the modern side; while those who are likely never to have any great use or aptitude for mathematics might also be allowed to rest, more or less, upon their oars. Generally speaking: whatsoever is *mere* apparatus may now be allowed to fall into the background, while the trained mind is gradually prepared for specialisation in the "subjects" which, when the Trivium is completed, it should be perfectly well equipped to tackle on its own. The final synthesis of the Trivium—the presentation and public defence of the thesis—should be restored in some form; perhaps as a kind of "leaving examination" during the last term at school.

The scope of Rhetoric depends also on whether the pupil is to be turned out into the world at the age of 16 or whether he is to proceed to public school and/or university. Since, really, Rhetoric should be taken at about 14, the first category of pupil should study Grammar from about

9 to 11, and Dialectic from 12 to 14; his last two school years would then be devoted to Rhetoric, which, in his case, would be of a fairly specialised and vocational kind, suiting him to enter immediately upon some practical career. A pupil of the second category would finish his Dialectical course in his Preparatory School, and take Rhetoric during his first two years at his Public School. At 16, he would be ready to start upon those "subjects" which are proposed for his later study at the university: and this part of his education will correspond to the mediaeval Quadrivium. What this amounts to is that the ordinary pupil, whose formal education ends at 16, will take the Trivium only; whereas scholars will take both Trivium and Quadrivium.

Is the Trivium, then, a sufficient education for life? Properly taught, I believe that it should be. At the end of the Dialectic, the children will probably seem to be far behind their coaevals brought up on old-fashioned "modern" methods, so far as detailed knowledge of specific subjects is concerned. But after the age of 14 they should be able to overhaul the others hand over fist. Indeed, I am not at all sure that a pupil thoroughly proficient in the Trivium would not be fit to proceed immediately to the university at the age of 16, thus proving himself the equal of his mediaeval counterpart, whose precocity astonished us at the beginning of this discussion. This, to be sure, would make hay of the public-school system, and disconcert the universities very much—it would, for example, make quite a different thing of the Oxford and Cambridge Boat-race. But I am not here to consider the feelings of academic bodies: I am concerned only with the proper training of the mind to encounter and deal with the formidable mass of undigested problems presented to it by the modern world. For the tools of learning are the same, in any and every subject; and the person who knows how to use them will, at any age, get the mastery of a new subject in half the time and with a quarter of the effort expended by the person who has not the tools at his command. To learn six subjects without remembering how they were learnt does nothing to ease the approach to a seventh; to have learnt and remembered the art of learning makes the approach to every subject an open door.

It is clear that the successful teaching of this neo-mediaeval curriculum will depend even more than usual upon the working together of the whole teaching staff towards a common purpose. Since no subject is considered as an end in itself, any kind of rivalry in the staff-room will be sadly out of place. The fact that a pupil is, unfortunately, obliged, for some reason, to miss the History period on Fridays, or the Shakespeare class on Tuesdays, or even to omit a whole subject in favour of some other subject, must not be allowed to cause any heart-burnings—the essential is that he should acquire the method of learning in whatever medium suits him best. If human nature suffers under this blow to one's professional pride in one's own subject, there is comfort in the thought that the end-of-term examination results will not be affected; for the papers will be so arranged as to be an examination in method, by whatever means.

I will add that it is highly important that every teacher should, for his or her own sake, be qualified and required to teach in all three parts of the Trivium; otherwise the Masters of Dialectic, especially, might find their minds hardening into a permanent adolescence. For this reason, teachers in Preparatory Schools should also take Rhetoric classes in the Public Schools to which they are attached; or, if they are not so attached, then by arrangement in other schools in the same neighbourhood. Alternatively, a few preliminary classes in Rhetoric might be taken in Preparatory Schools from the age of 13 onwards.

Before concluding these necessarily very sketchy suggestions, I ought to say why I think it necessary, in these days, to go back to a discipline which we had discarded. The truth is that for the last 300 years or so we have been living upon our educational capital. The post-renaissance world, bewildered and excited by the profusion of new "subjects" offered to it, broke away from the old discipline (which had, indeed, become sadly dull and stereotyped in its practical application) and imagined that henceforward it could, as it were, disport itself happily in its new and extended quadrivium without passing through the trivium. But the scholastic tradition, though broken and maimed, still lingered in the public schools and universities: Milton, however much he protested against it, was formed by it—the debate of the fallen angels, and the disputation of abdiel with Satan have the tool-marks of the schools upon them, and might, incidentally, profitably figure as set passages for our dialectical studies. Right down to the 19th century, our public affairs were mostly managed, and our books and journals were for the most part written, by people brought up in homes, and trained in places, where that tradition was still alive in the memory and almost in the blood. Just so, many people to-day who are atheist or agnostic in religion, are governed in their conduct by a code of Christian ethics which is so rooted in their unconscious assumptions that it never occurs to them to question it. But one cannot live on capital for ever. A tradition, however firmly rooted, if it is never watered, though it dies hard, yet in the end it dies. And today a great number—perhaps the majority—of the men and women who handle our affairs, write our books and our newspapers, carry out research, present our plays and our films, speak from our platforms and pulpits—yes, and who educate our young people, have never, even in a lingering traditional memory, undergone the scholastic discipline. Less and less do the children who come to be educated bring any of that tradition with them. We have lost the tools of learning--the axe and the wedge, the hammer and the saw, the chisel and the plane--that were so adaptable to all tasks. Instead of them, we have merely a set of complicated jigs, each of which will do but one task and no more, and in using which eye and hand receive no training, so that no man ever sees the work as a whole or "looks to the end of the work." what use is it to pile task on task and prolong the days of labour, if at the close the chief object is left unattained? It is not the fault of the teachers--they work only too hard already. The combined folly of a civilisation that has forgotten its own roots is forcing them to shore up the tottering weight of an educational structure that is built upon sand. They are doing for their pupils the work which the pupils themselves ought to do. For the sole true end of education is simply this: to teach men how to learn for themselves; and whatever instruction fails to do this is effort spent in vain.

Appendix 2

DISCUSSION AS A MEANS OF TEACHING AND LEARNING[1]

What follows is a description of a St. John's Seminar.

A book or a part of it is to be discussed; about twenty students (usually fewer and seldom more) sit around a table, and two tutors have to act as moderators of the discussion. The students are supposed to have read the book or the assigned part of it before coming to the seminar. Some have done that well and thoroughly, some not well and superficially; it may even happen that a student has not read the book at all. One of the tutors begins the discussion by raising a question, directly related to what is said in the book. Sometimes a silence ensues before a student chooses to answer the question; sometimes the answer follows the question immediately. This answer may provoke a comment or a refutation or a new question coming from students or tutors. Thus an exchange of opinions develops, which can be animated, even heated, or calm and slow. Quite a few students participate in this exchange, while some remain silent.

What happens while this exchange goes on? Many things. What the book is about may be clarified to some extent. How its content is connected with the content of other books may be discovered, weighed or subtly suggested. But more important things do occur. A student might find his most cherished thought elucidated or his most burdensome question answered in the book, and this gives him the opportunity to bring about a discussion of this favorite theme of his, which turns the seminar away from the book altogether. And yet, what is then being

[1] The complete text of Jacob Klein, "Discussion as a Means of Teaching and Learning," *The College* (1971): 1–2 is reprinted here by the permission of St. John's College. St. John's College Digital Archives, accessed 2024 August 1: https://digitalarchives.sjc.edu/items/show/452.

discussed may be something more fundamental for the understanding of one's world and one's life. Or, on the contrary, a student may see for the first time that something he had always accepted is actually highly doubtful. A sentence, even a single word, uttered by one of the participants in the discussion, may open to him a new vista, may challenge his deepest convictions, may aggravate the awareness of his ignorance.

It is thus that learning takes place, not in the sense that the students are being "informed" about opinions and doctrines uttered in the books, about events and facts mentioned in them, about plots and stories presented and narrated. What is achieved is rather an expansion of the intellectual horizon, a fostering of understanding, a demolition of false assumptions. This may not happen at all in any one seminar or even in a series of seminars; but it is likely to happen after a while, which means that only a steady continuation of the seminars through a lengthy period of time makes the seminar exercises fruitful and beneficial.

Two fundamental rules determine the discussion. As the College catalogue puts it: "every opinion must be heard and explored, however sharp the clash of opinions may be," and "every opinion must be supported by argument—an unsupported opinion does not count." But it is not possible to avoid empty or even frivolous talk altogether. Serious arguments may degenerate into repetitious and shallow assertions. It is the task of the moderators, the seminar leaders, to turn the discussion back to its meaningful origin. They are not always able to do that because even wasteful and extravagant claims might contain points that fascinate the students' imagination and stimulate their urge to refute and to explore. Even then learning may take place.

Very rarely is a question fully answered and the answer approved by all present. The main purpose of the seminar is not to find final solutions of perennial problems, but to become aware of a range of possible answers. Nor is it the purpose of the seminar to interpret the content of a book once and for all. Be it Homer or Virgil or Dante or Shakespeare, be it Plato or Aristotle or Descartes or Kant, be it Thucydides or Augustine or Hegel, be it any other author, none of the students and tutors is expected to "master" any one of their works, but everyone is expected to discover the diversity of possible interpretations that these works give rise to and the depth of the task that understanding them presents.

Some troublesome aspects of the seminar have to be mentioned. There is too much to read, and the riches of the books are overwhelming. The habits of the students, as far as reading, listening, and arguing are concerned, vary to a very great extent. This can make the discussion uneasy or turbulent or even explosive. It is, at any rate, always unpredictable, as indeed it should be. But there is always the possibility that some spoken word—or some word withheld—may provoke a student with an insight of a penetrating nature, not necessarily related to the book or topic under discussion. The occurrence of learning itself is indeed unpredictable.

One indispensable—although not always sufficient—condition must prevail for learning to occur. It is the effort on the part of students, a continuous effort, to find answers to the questions raised. The answer to the question what learning itself is, is not a "theory of knowledge," a so-called "epistemology," but the very effort to learn. That is why in Plato's *Meno* Socrates keeps exhorting Meno and the young slave to "make an attempt" to answer. And that is why, in Plato's *Republic* (376B), Glaucon has to agree with Socrates that the "love of learning" (τὸ φιλομαθής) and the "love of wisdom" (τὸ φιλόσοφον) are the same. This "love of learning," which leads to the effort to learn, may not result in actual learning—it may indeed be insufficient, just as the "love of wisdom" may not result ln obtaining wisdom and knowledge. The pursuit of understanding and of knowledge in the seminar is clouded by this uncertainty and unpredictability. But at some point of the discussion some understanding may be gained by some student or students, and this understanding may then evolve further and further. Let us also bear in mind that this point may never be reached.

In what then does teaching consist in a St. John's seminar? Certainly not in the "pouring" of knowledge into the learner's soul, just as learning does not consist in listening and repeating what one has heard. It is hard for any tutor to resist the temptation to present his own opinions about the content of a book or about the hidden meaning of a phrase. Sometimes such a presentation may even be fruitful because it can provoke counter-argument and far-reaching discussion. Above all, however, the seminar leaders have to solicit the opinions of the students, to try to keep the discussion within the limits of the subject argued about, which is not at all easy, and to let the students participate as much as possible in the debate. Not seldom some students remain altogether silent, and it may become important to the tutors to understand the nature of this silence by talking to these students outside of the seminar. Conversations between tutor and student outside of the seminar are, of course, generally most desirable and helpful.

As to the "silent" students, their silence can ultimately be attributed to two very different causes. One is a lack of interest which implies the absence of that effort to learn, on which so much depends. If this attitude of the student persists and cannot be broken, it is not likely that the student will continue to be a student. The other cause is a deep and complex involvement in what is read and said, so deep and complex, in fact, that the student cannot afford to take a stand and to open his mouth, because he would have to say too many things at once. This student listens attentively, and his inside effort to clear his thoughts, by separating what does not belong together and by combining what does, may lead him to learn a great deal. Here again it is not possible to predict whether this learning will occur. But when it does, it is bountiful and precious.

www.ingramcontent.com/pod-product-compliance
Lightning Source LLC
Chambersburg PA
CBHW070037100426
42740CB00013B/2712
* 9 7 8 1 6 3 6 6 3 1 1 1 0 *